Drumbo Ontario and Area in Colour Photos, Saving Our History One Photo at a Time

Photography by Barbara Raué
© 2019 updated

Series Name: Cruising Ontario

Book 44: Drumbo and other Blandford-Blenheim Township Towns

Cover photo: Drumbo House c. 1880, Page 17

© 2018 by Barbara Raue - All the photos in this book have been taken with my cameras. I own the rights to them.

Series Name: Cruising Ontario
Saving Our History One Photo at a Time
in colour photos

Towns in Alphabetical Order:
Aberfoyle, Acton, Alton, Amherstburg, Ancaster, Arthur, Auburn, Aylmer, Ayr, Beaver Valley, Belgrave, Belleville, Bloomingdale, Blyth, Brantford, Brockville, Burford, Burlington, Caledon, Caledonia, Cambridge, Carlow, Chatsworth, Clifford, Collingwood, Conestogo, Delhi, Dorchester to Aylmer, Drayton, Drumbo, Dundas, Dunlop, Eden Mills, Elmira, Elora, Erin, Essex, Fergus, Goderich, Grimsby, Guelph, Hagersville, Hamilton, Hanover, Harriston, Hespeler, Jarvis, Kingston, Kingsville, Kitchener, Lake Superior, Lincoln, Linwood, Listowel, London, Lucknow, Merrickville, Mono, Mount Forest, Mount Pleasant, Neustadt, New Hamburg, Newboro, Newport, Niagara-on-the-Lake, Oakville, Onondaga, Orangeville, Orillia, Owen Sound, Palmerston, Paris, Pelham, Perth, Peterborough, Petrolia, Port Colborne, Port Elgin, Portland, Preston, Rockwood, Sarnia, Sault Ste. Marie, Seaforth, Sheffield, Shelburne, Simcoe, Smiths Falls, Smithville, Southampton, St. Catharines, St. George, St. Jacobs, St. Marys, St. Thomas, Stoney Creek, Stratford, Thamesford, Thunder Bay, Tillsonburg, Toronto, Waterdown, Waterford, Waterloo, Welland, Wellesley, Westport, Windsor, Wingham, Woodstock

Book 196: Pelham
Book 197: Beaver Valley
Book 198: Chatsworth
Book 199: Wingham

Table of Contents

Drumbo	Page 5
Princeton	Page 20
Etonia	Page 35
Gobles	Page 36
Richwood	Page 37
Wolverton	Page 38
Washington	Page 40
Plattsville	Page 47
Bright	Page 58
Windfall	Page 68
Ratho	Page 69
Architectural Terms	Page 70
Building Styles	Page 72

Drumbo acquired its name in 1852; the community was named after Drumbo, Ireland. It is located in Blandford-Blenheim Township, Oxford County at the crossroads of County Road #3 (Wilmot Street) and County Road #29 (Oxford Street); this is south of the 401 Highway and 24 kilometers northeast of Woodstock.

Princeton is located in Oxford County on Country Road #3, twenty-two kilometers east of Woodstock. Etonia, east of Princeton, and Gobles, west of Princeton, are both located on County Road 2. Richwood is located on Blenheim Road and Township Road 5, north of Etonia.

The village of Wolverton is named after its founder, Enos Wolverton (1810-1893), who built up a successful milling enterprise on the Nith River. Enos came to Upper Canada with his parents from Cayuga County, New York state in 1826. He married Harriet Towl in 1834 and had two daughters, Roseltha (Rose) and Melissa (Lissa), and five sons, Alfred, Daniel, Alonzo, Jasper and Newton. Enos' brother, Asa Wolverton, became a successful businessman in nearby Paris, Ontario. The Crimean War (1854-1856) brought on an agricultural boom in Upper Canada and increased the Wolvertons' fortunes.

Washington is on County Road 3 (Washington Road) and Regional Road 8, east of Plattsville and north of Drumbo.

Plattsville is located on Township Road 13 & 42 (Albert Street) and Regional Road 8. It is located north of Highway 401, and 32 kilometers northeast of Woodstock. The community was named for its founder, Edward Platt, who settled in 1811 and built a flour mill.

Bright is located where County Roads 22 and 8 cross. Windfall is located on Oxford Road 29, north of Highway 401, west of Drumbo, south of Bright.

Ratho is located on Blandford Road and Township Road 13, northwest of Bright.

Drumbo

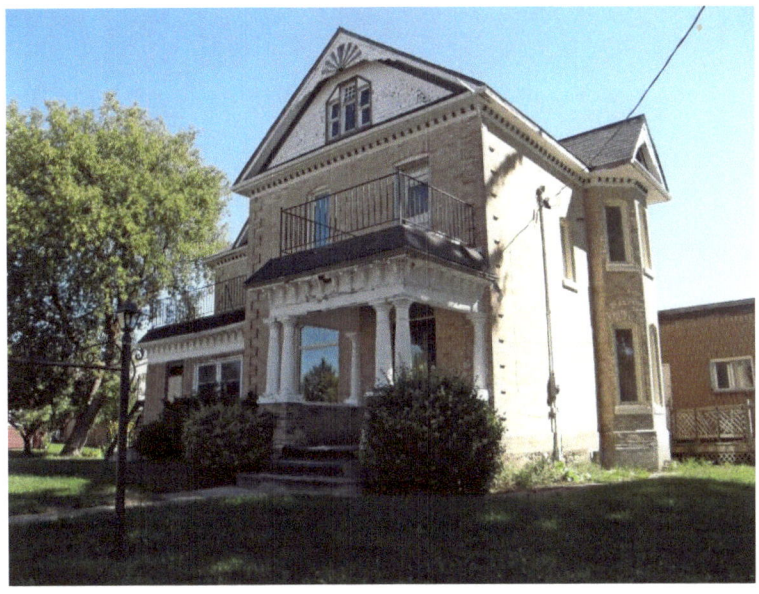

Yellow brick, Ionic style pillars supporting an upper balcony

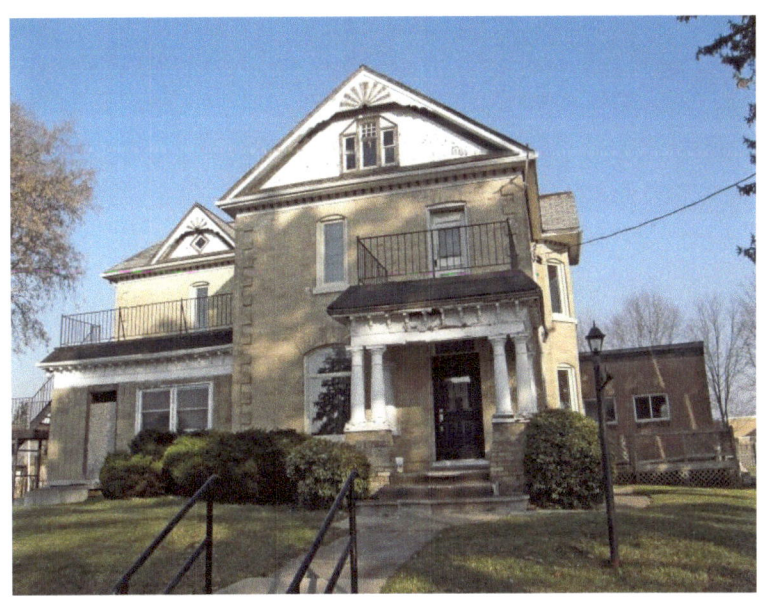

Decorated gables - Gothic Revival style

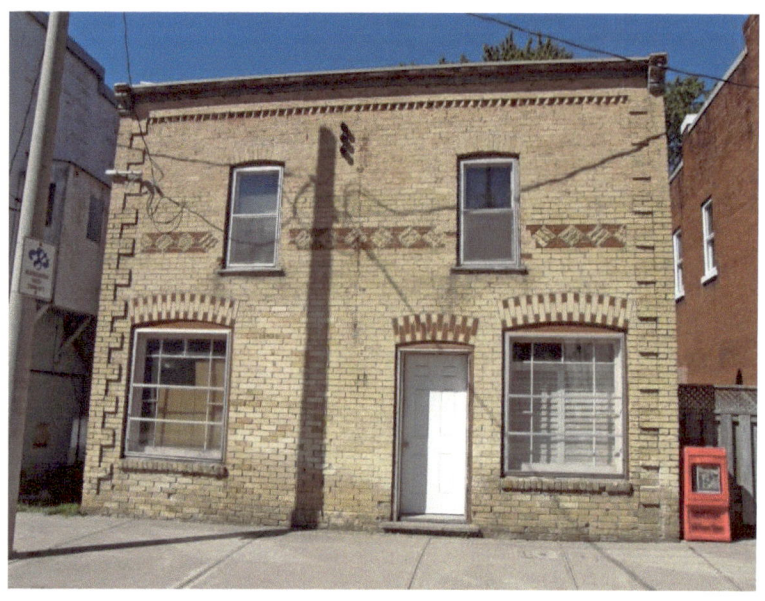

Dichromatic brickwork with two colours of brick for decoration, voussoirs, corner quoins

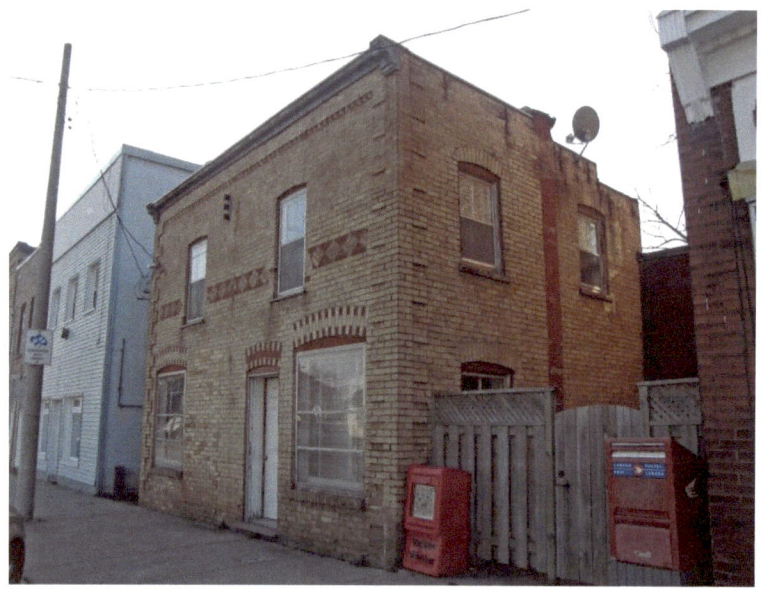

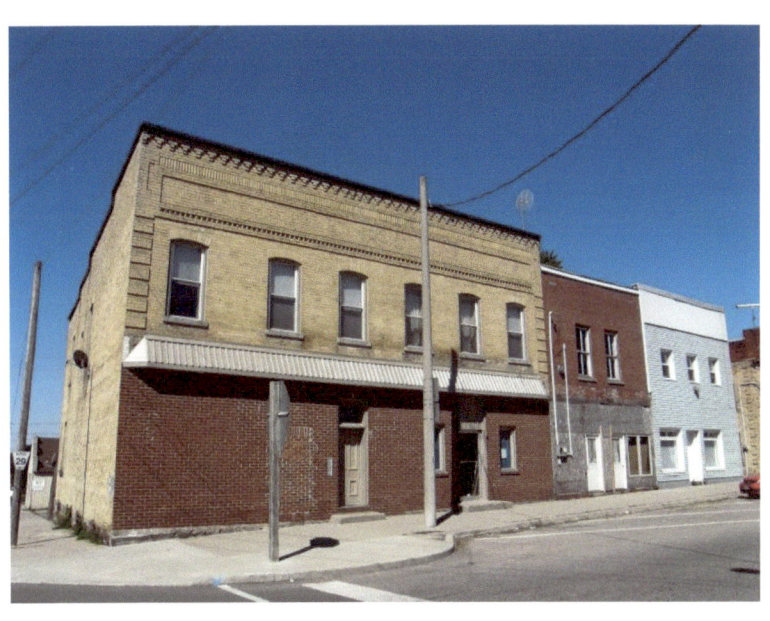

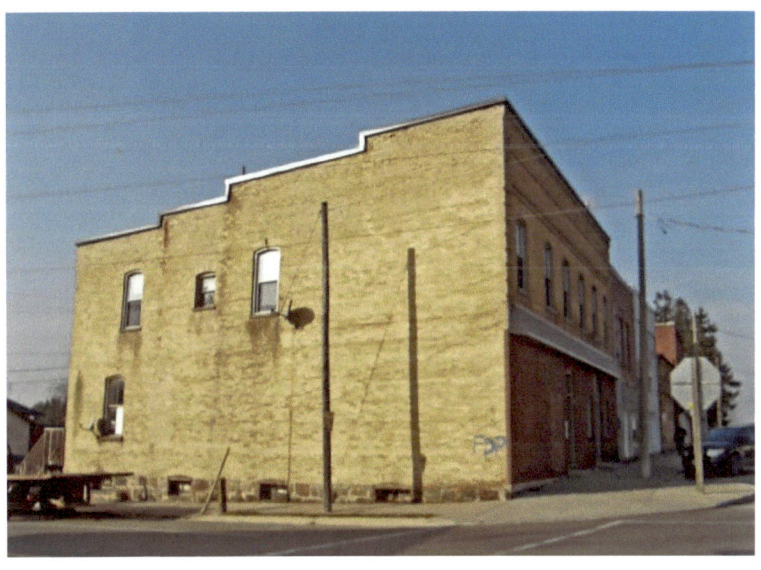

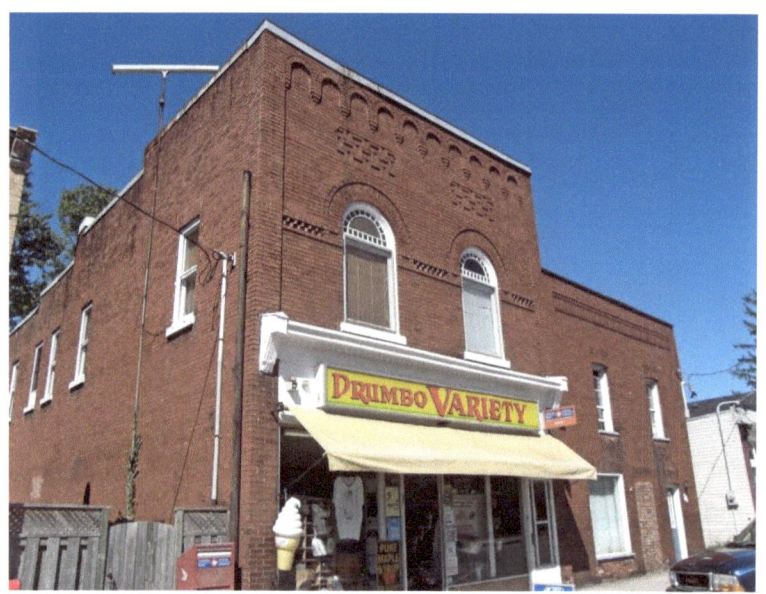

24 Wilmot Street North - Renaissance Revival storefront

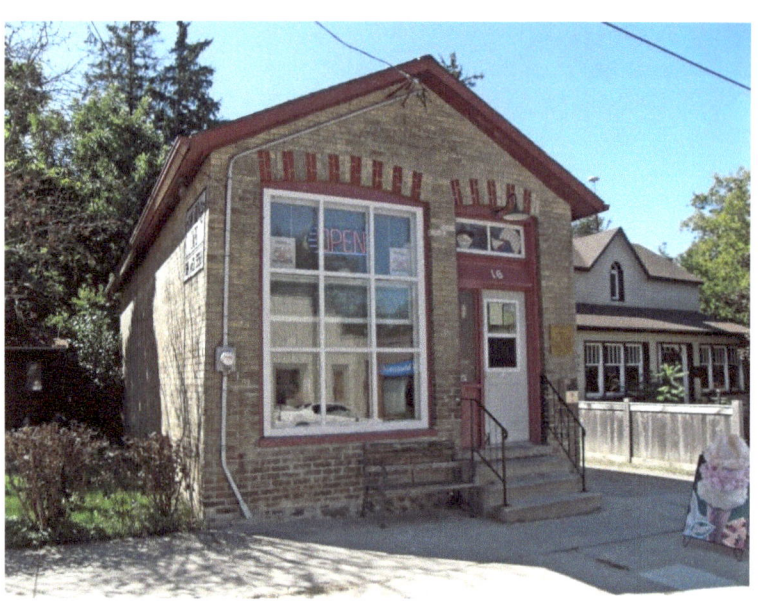

Decorated with a second colour of brick
#16

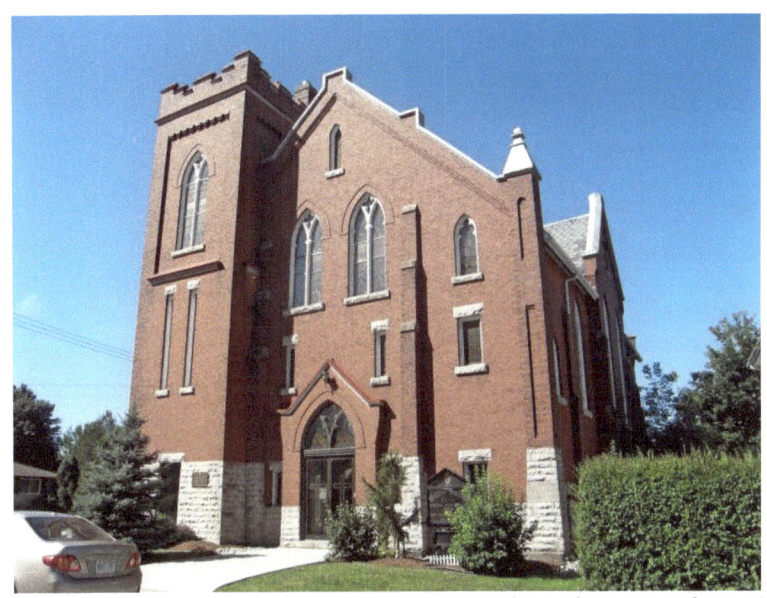

15 Centre Street - Drumbo Presbyterian Church erected 1869, rebuilt 1915 - now Willis United Church – battlement, buttresses, lancet windows

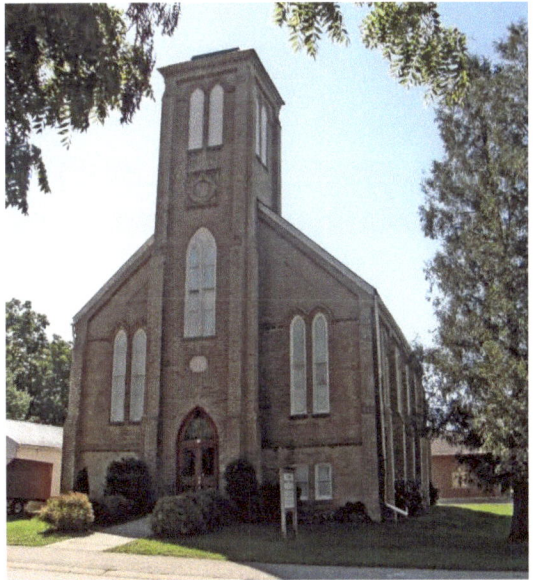

20 Pinkham Street - Drumbo Baptist Church, A.D. 1876 – lancet windows, three storey tower, buttresses

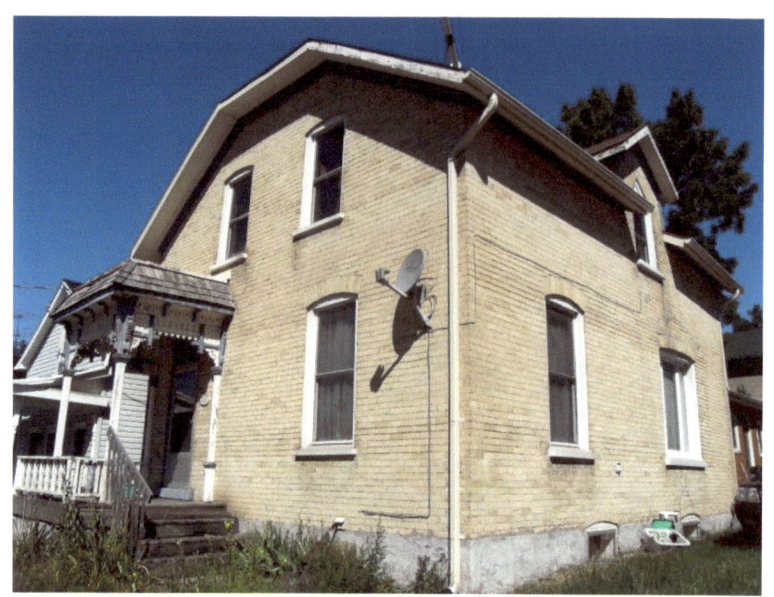
#25 – chipped front gable

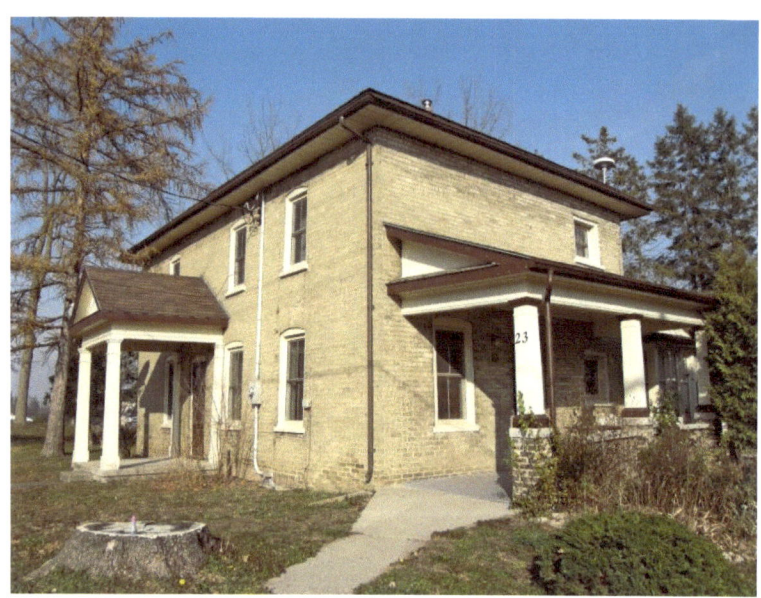
#23 – hip roof

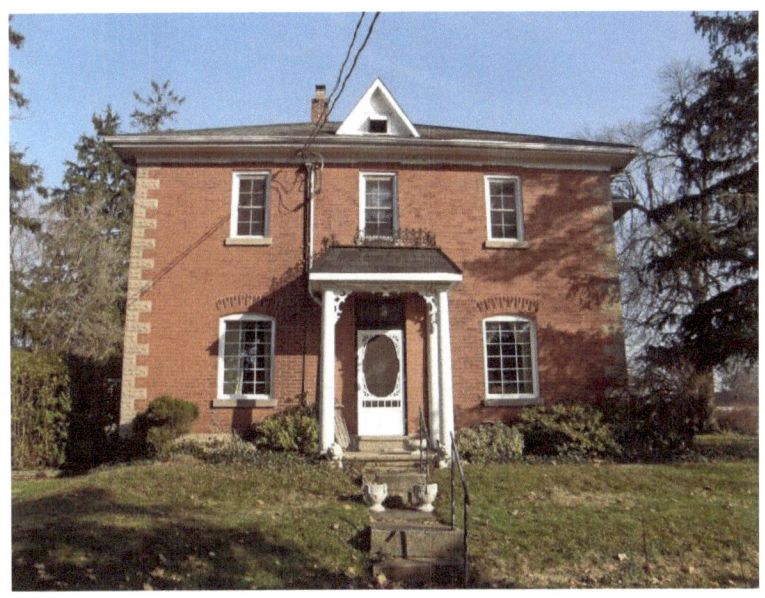

Corner quoins, voussoirs, iron cresting around second floor balcony

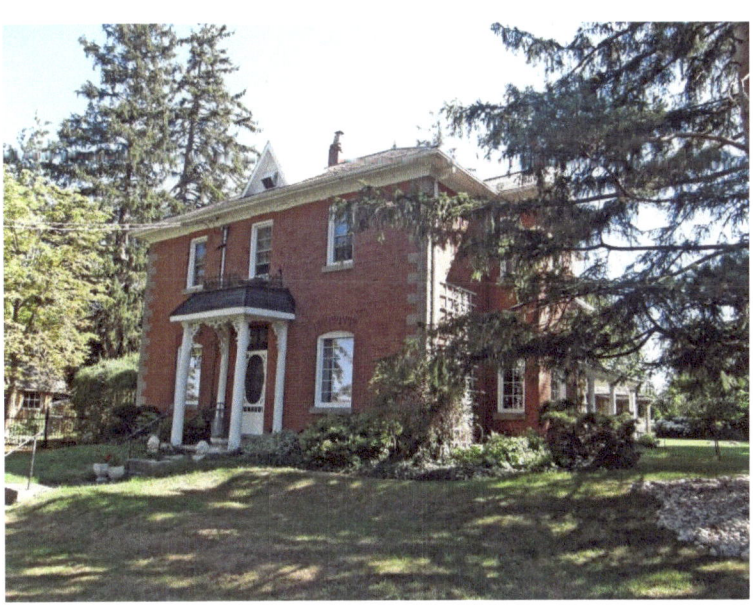

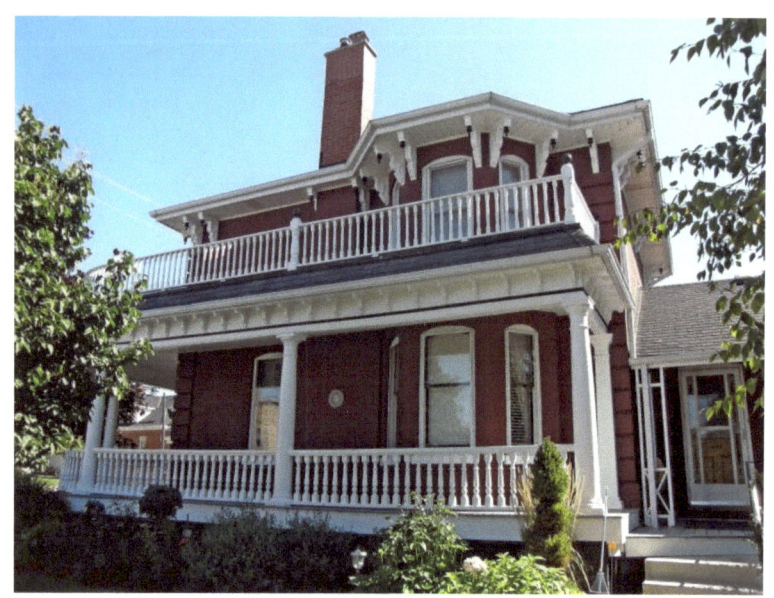

Cornice brackets, two-storey veranda

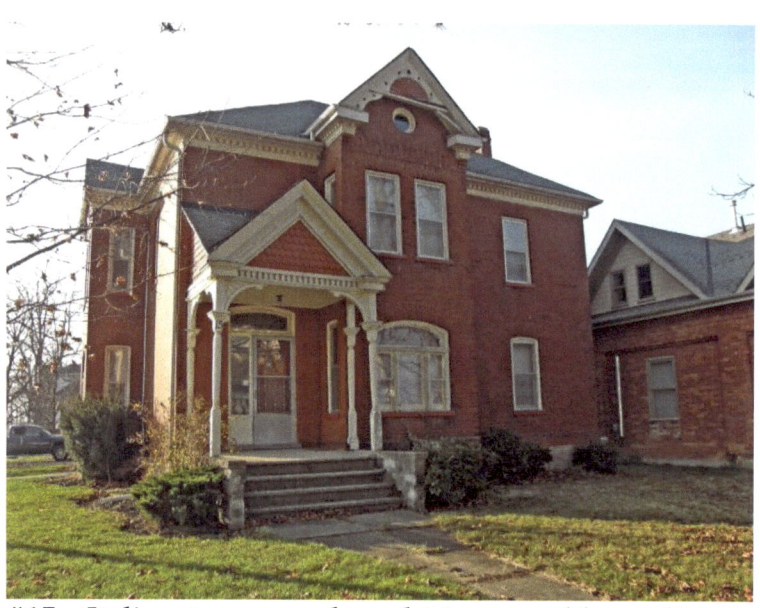

#15 – Italianate – verge board trim on gable, pediment

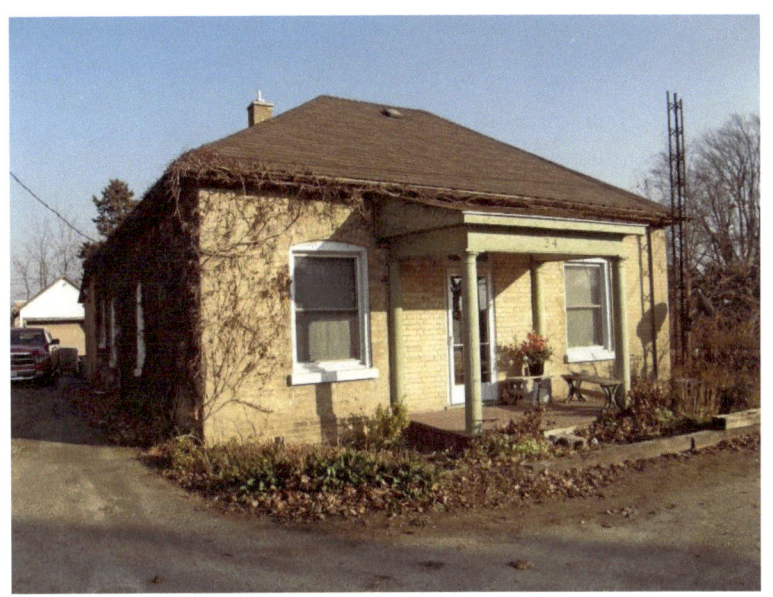

#24 – Regency brick cottage

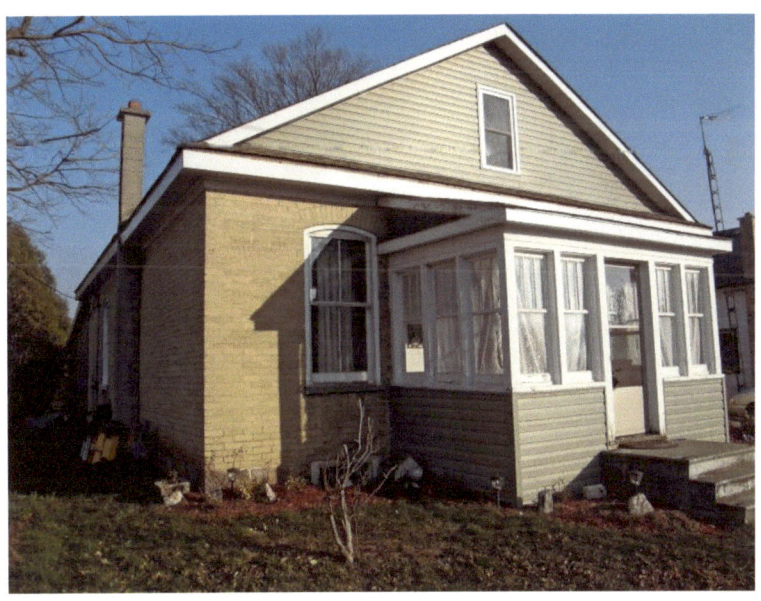

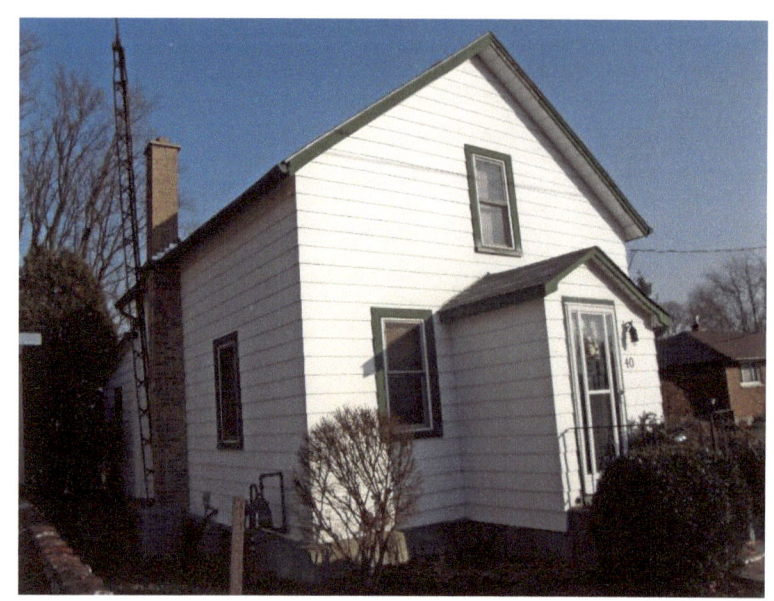

#40

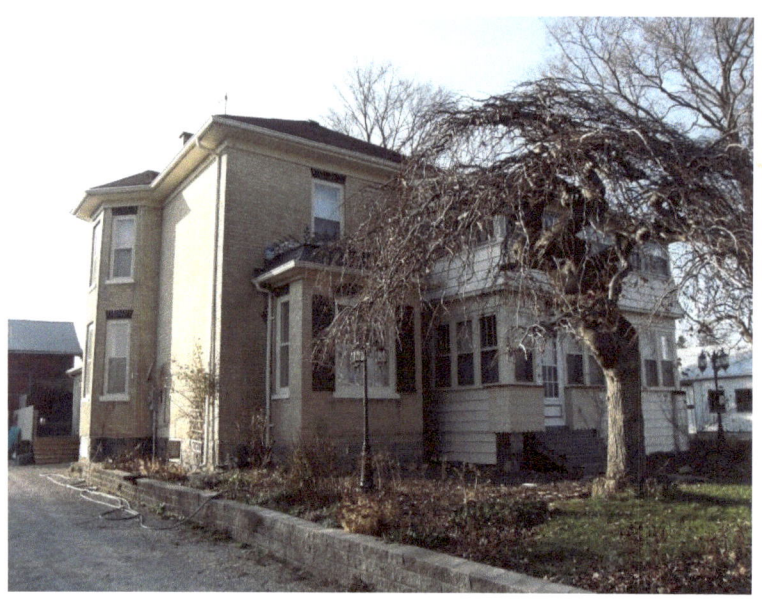

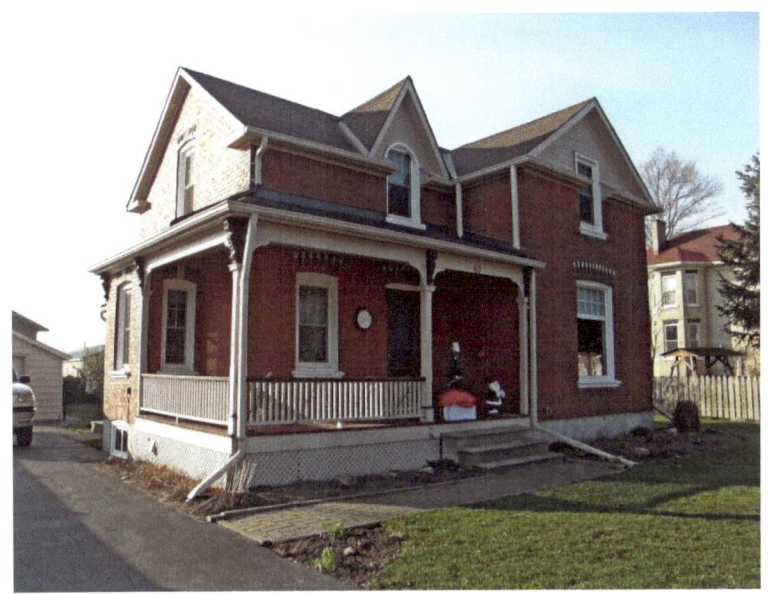

43 Oxford Street – Gothic

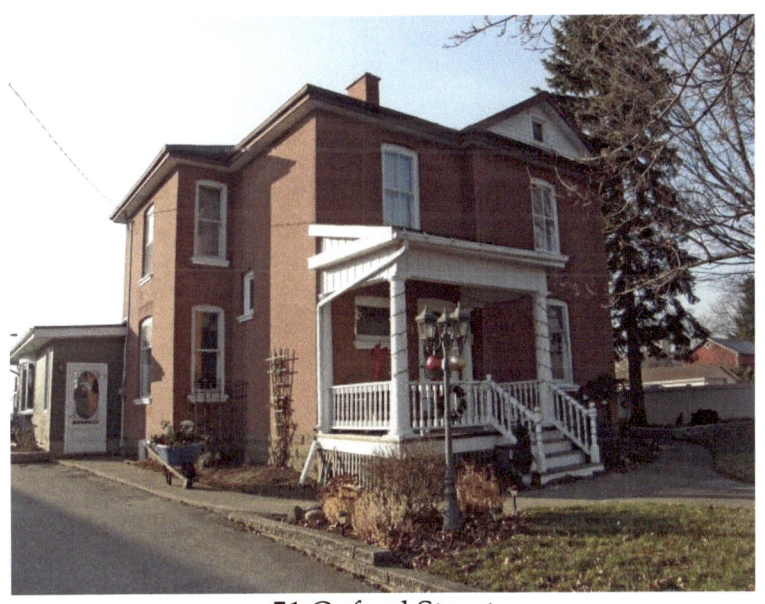

51 Oxford Street

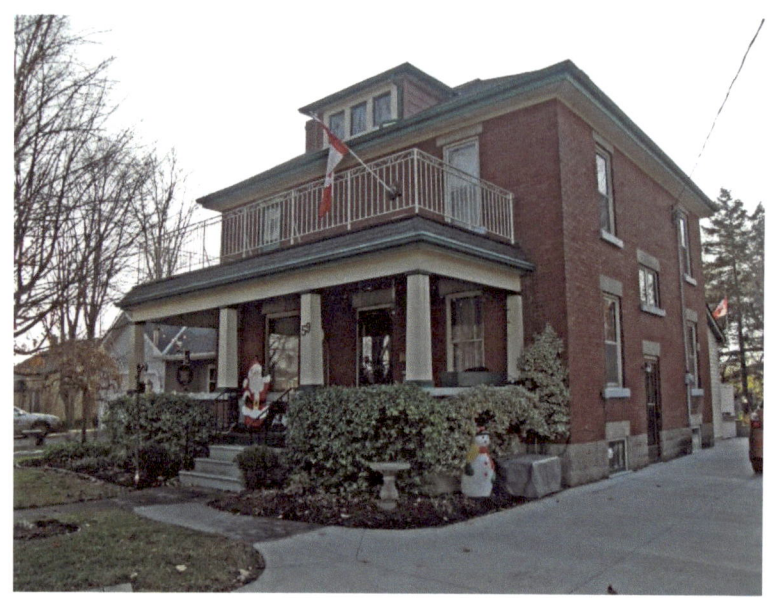

59 Oxford Street - balcony above the veranda, dormer window

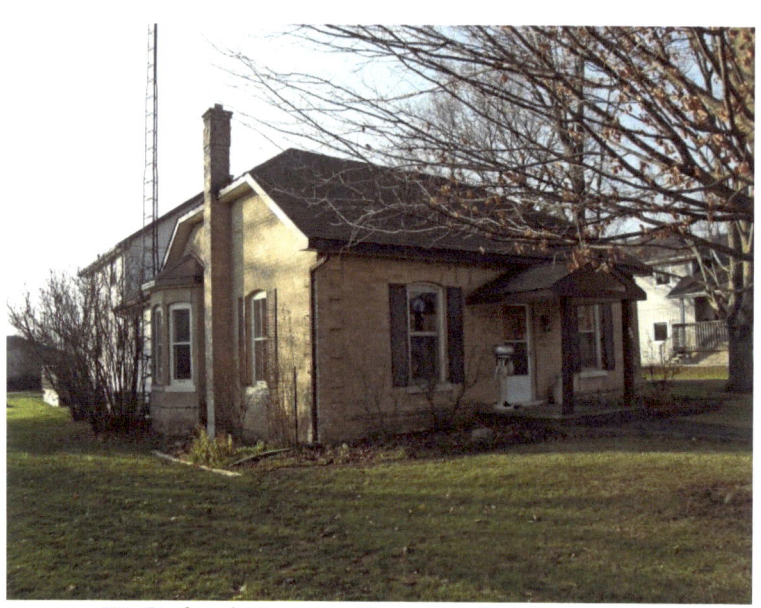

75 Oxford Street – Regency brick cottage

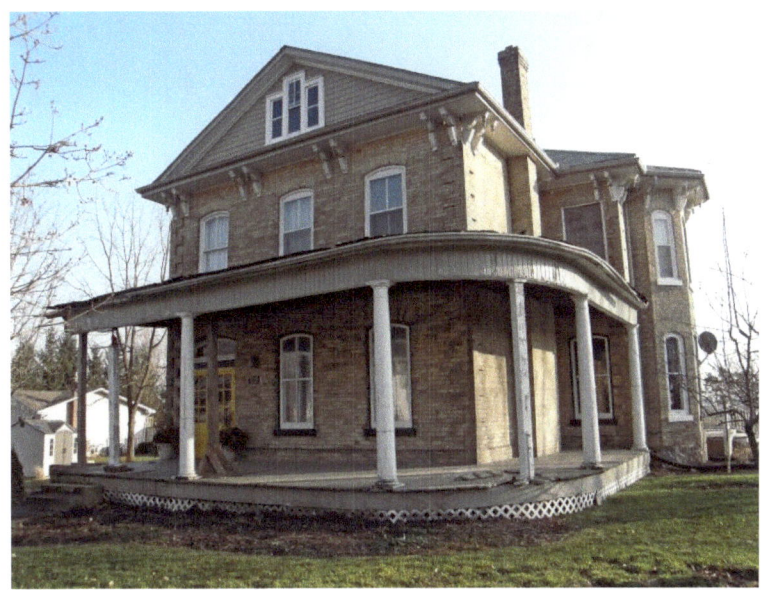

23 Oxford Street - Prominent brackets on the cornice (roof overhang), triangular pediment above with a Palladian type triple window in the tympanum with the centre window flanked by two lower windows

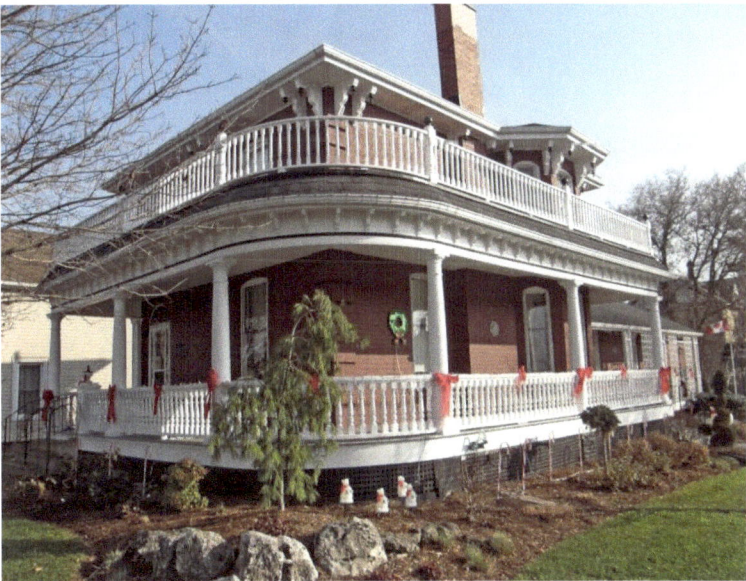

c. 1880 - wraparound two-storey veranda, cornice brackets

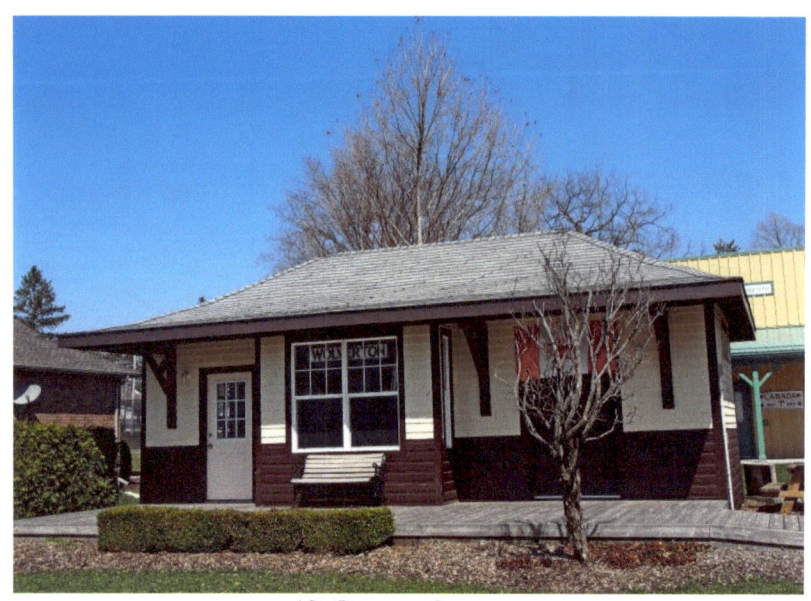

42 Centre Street -

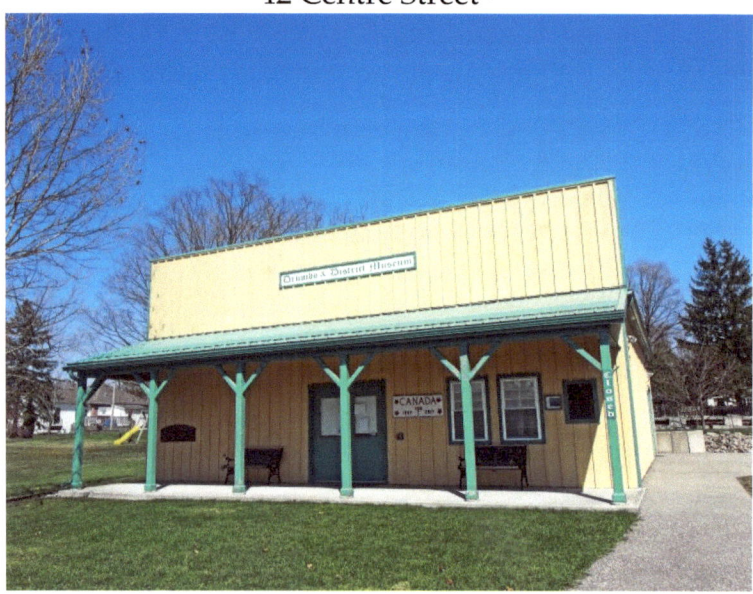

42 Centre Street - Drumbo & District Museum – Muma Block – 1890 – Henry Muma was a farmer, land agent, and entrepreneur; he built a sawmill and had a brickmaking business.

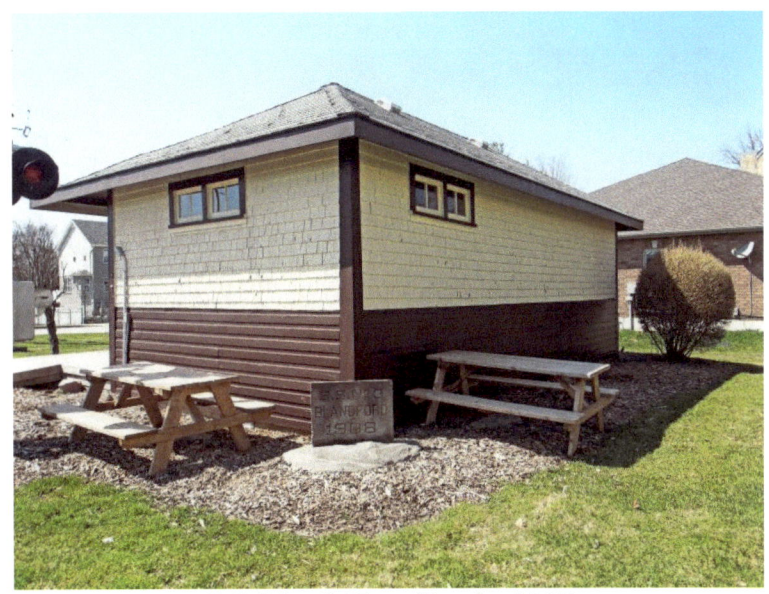

S.S. No. 3 Blandford - 1908

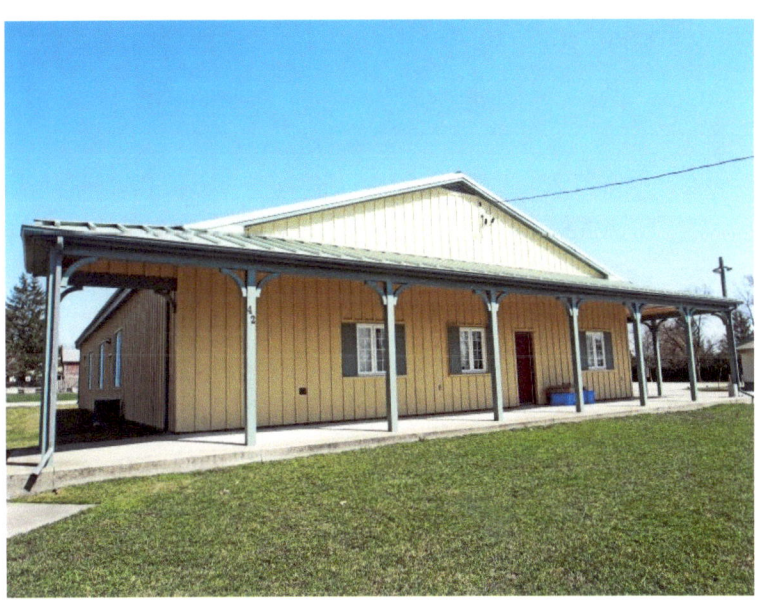

Princeton

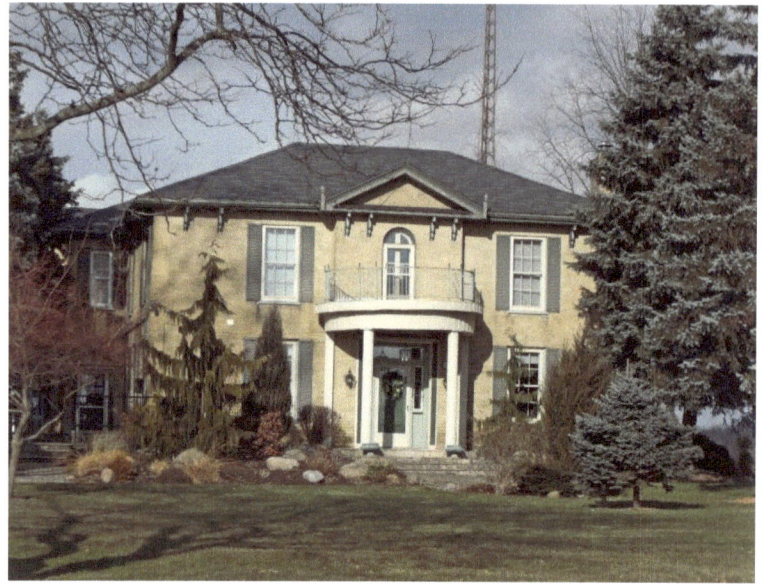

Neo-Classical style - hip roof, cornice brackets, semi-circular balcony above front door with sidelights and transom

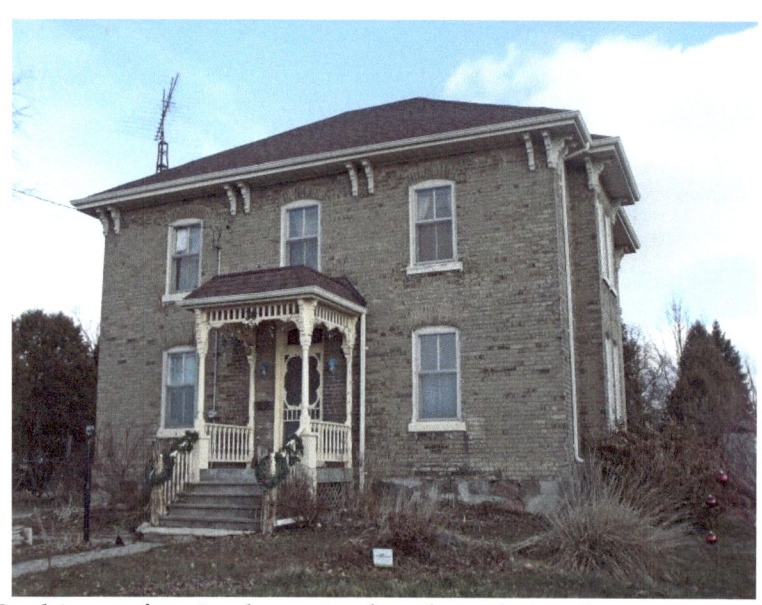

#30 – hip roof, paired cornice brackets, bric-a-brac on veranda

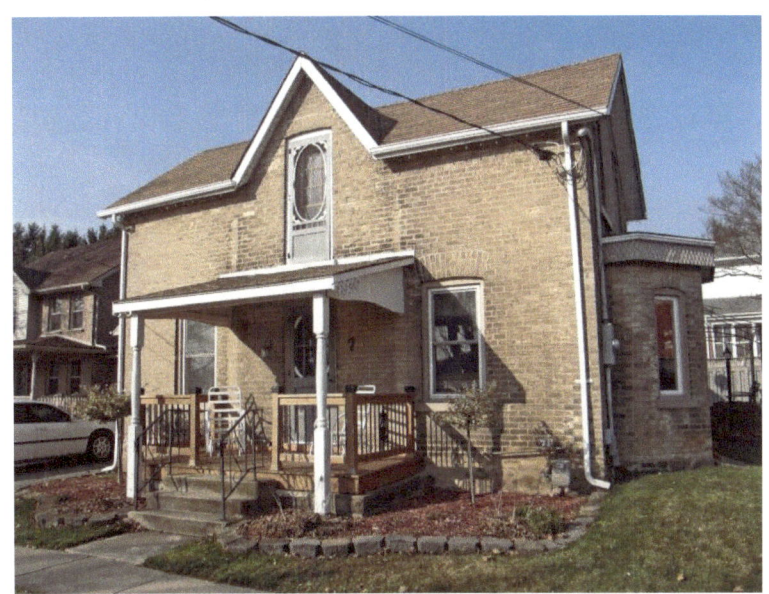

7 Elgin Street - Gothic

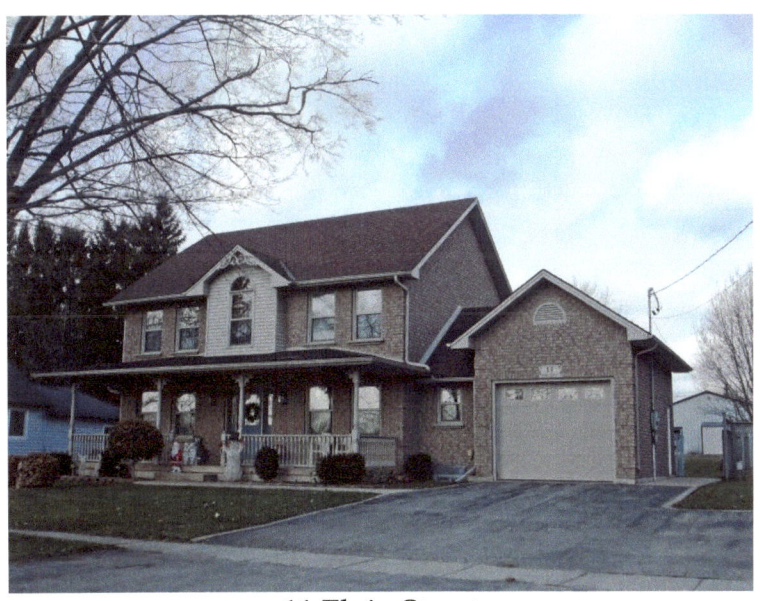

11 Elgin Street

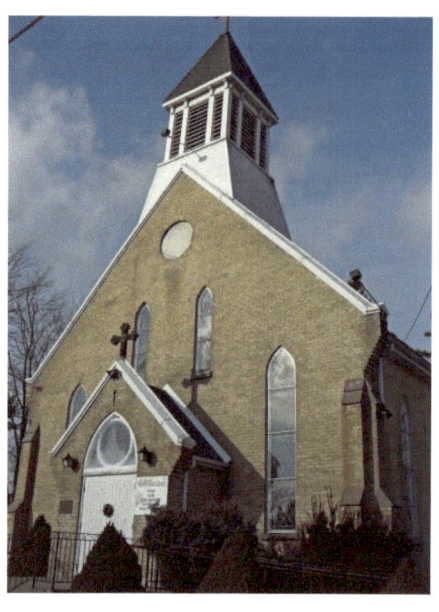

Sacred Heart Church established 1888 – cupola, lancet windows, buttresses

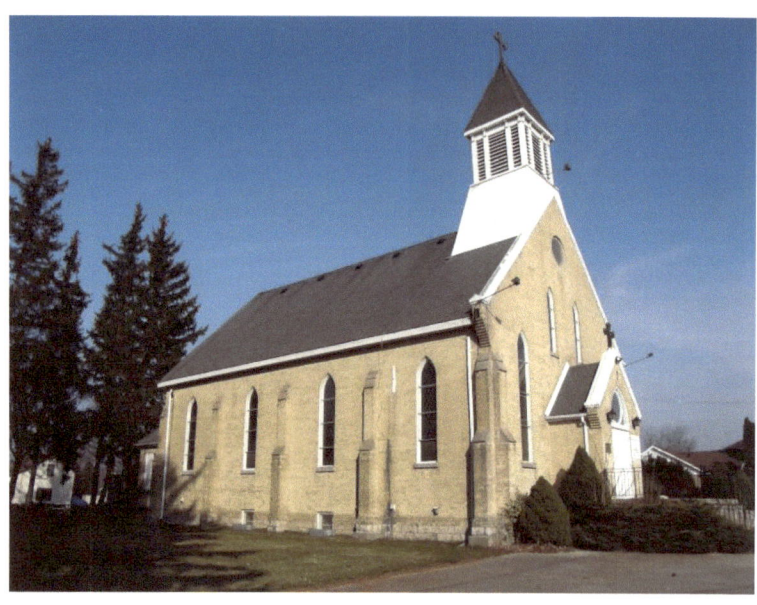

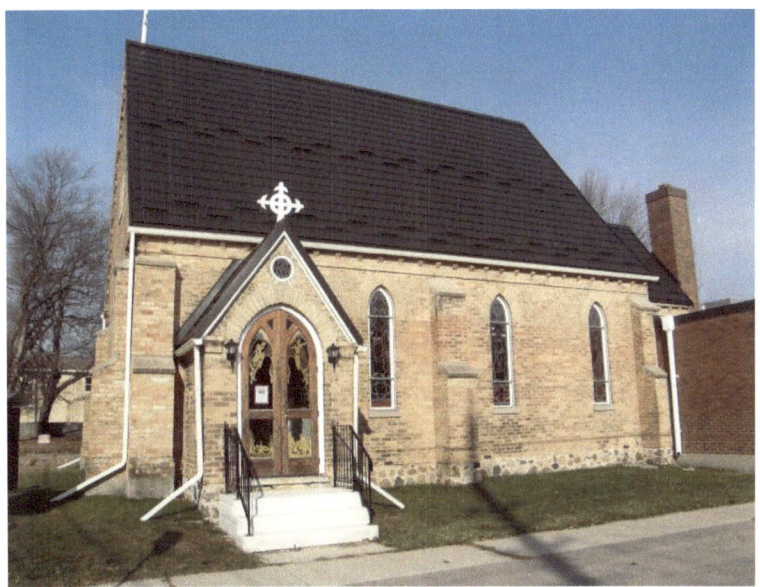

4 Elgin Street East, corner of Main Street - St. Paul's Anglican Church – built in 1867, restored 1917 – buttresses, lancet windows

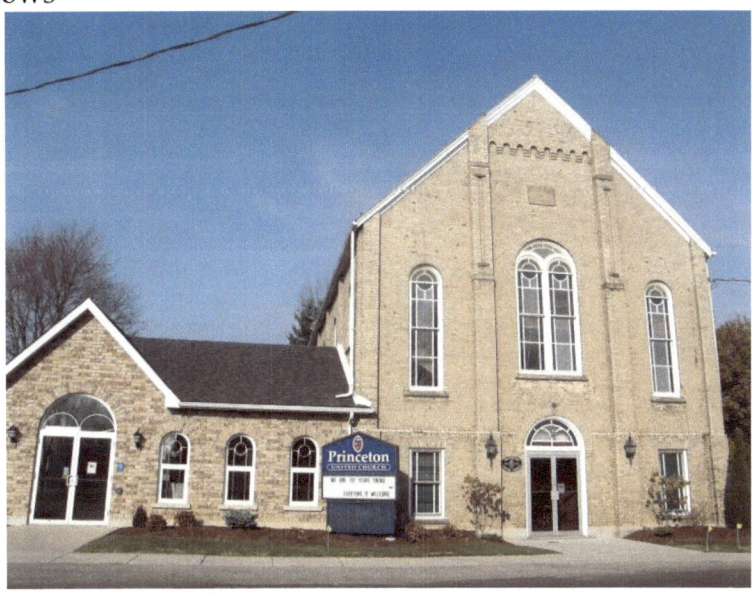

Elgin Street - originally Methodist Church – 1880 - now Princeton United Church

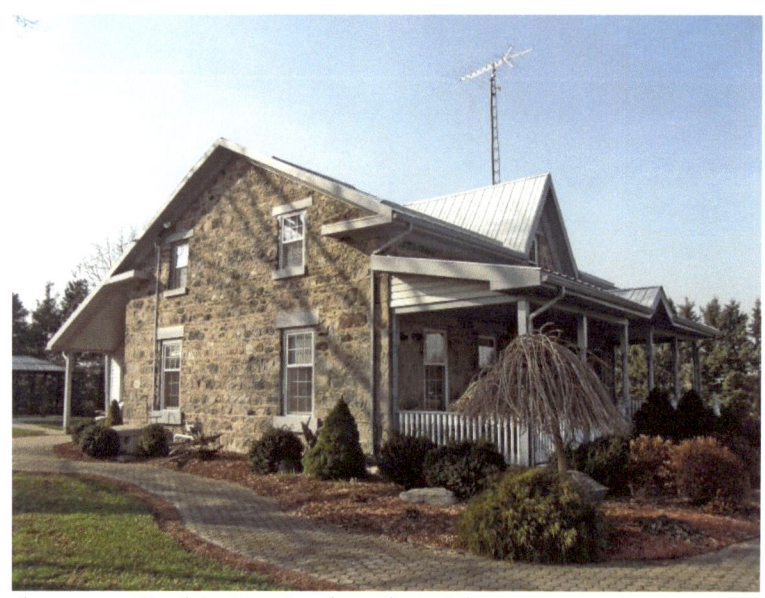

Stone house – Gothic Revival style with center arch, cornice return on gable which was popular in Neo-classical Ontario architecture

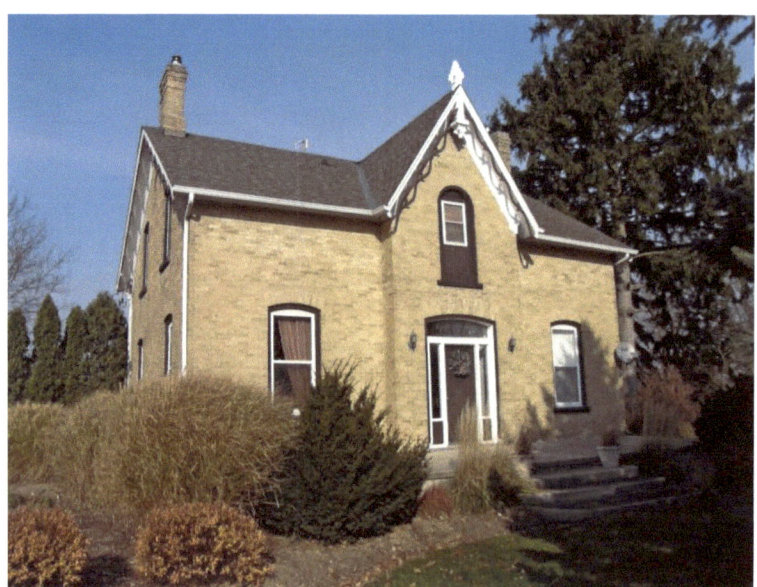

Gothic Revival style with gingerbread verge board and finial

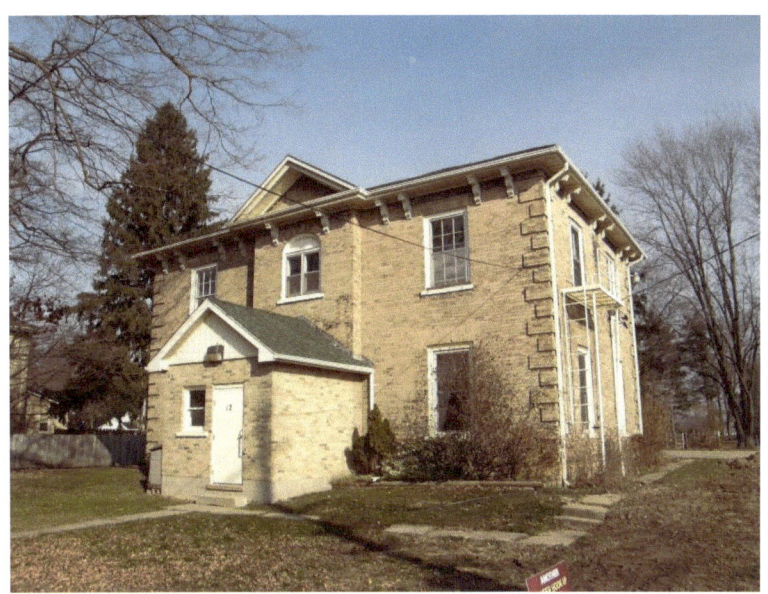

#12 - cornice brackets, corner quoins

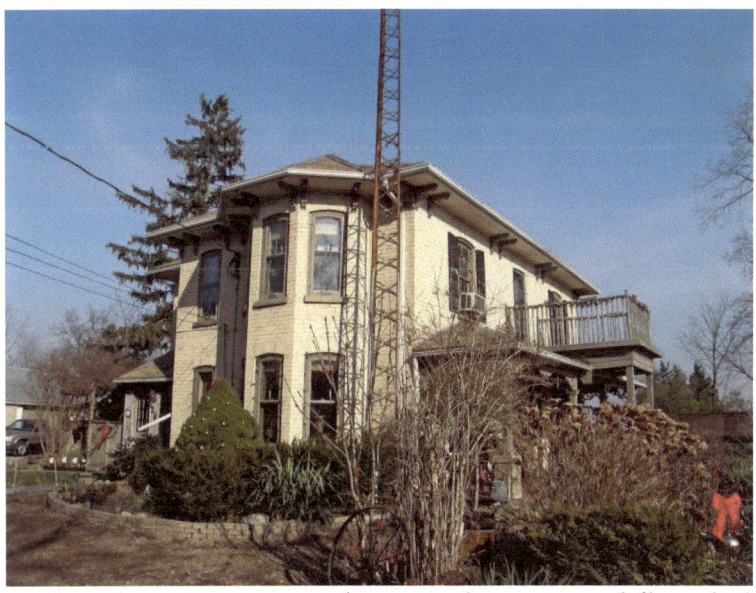

Cornice brackets, two-storey bay window, second floor balcony

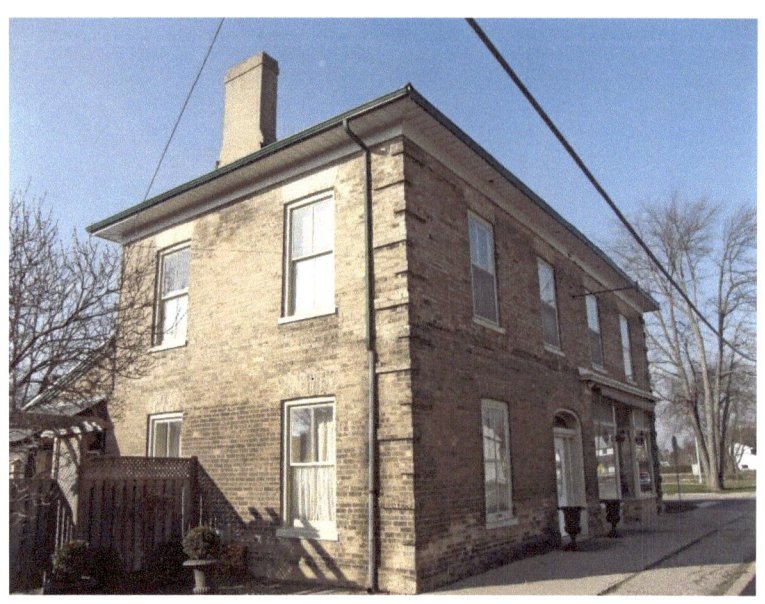

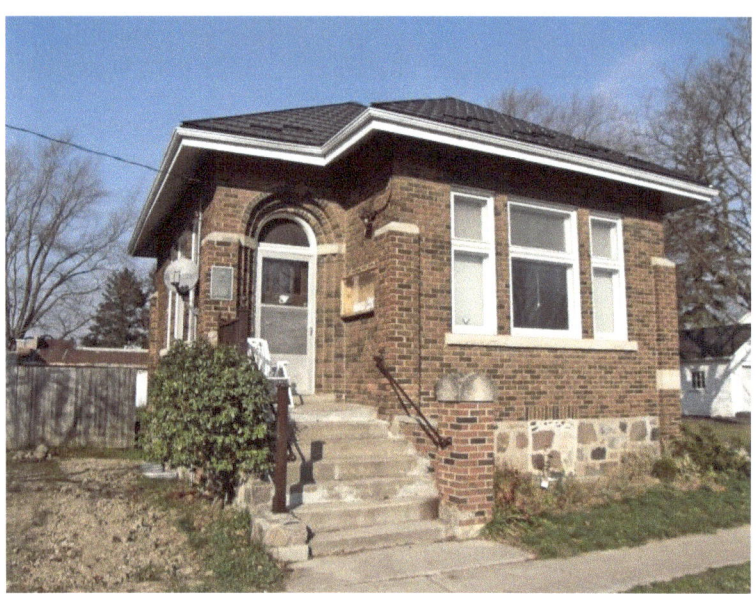

Branch of Oxford County Library plaque - House built in 1921 – hip roof, banding

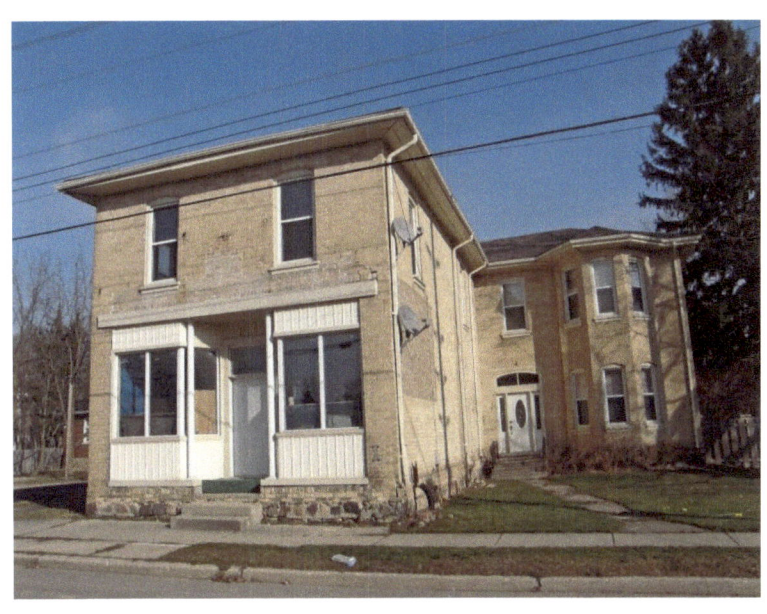
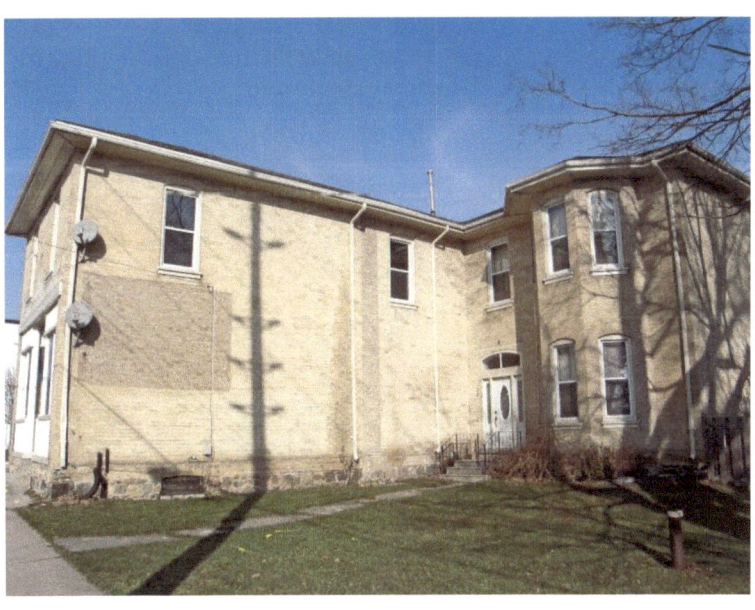

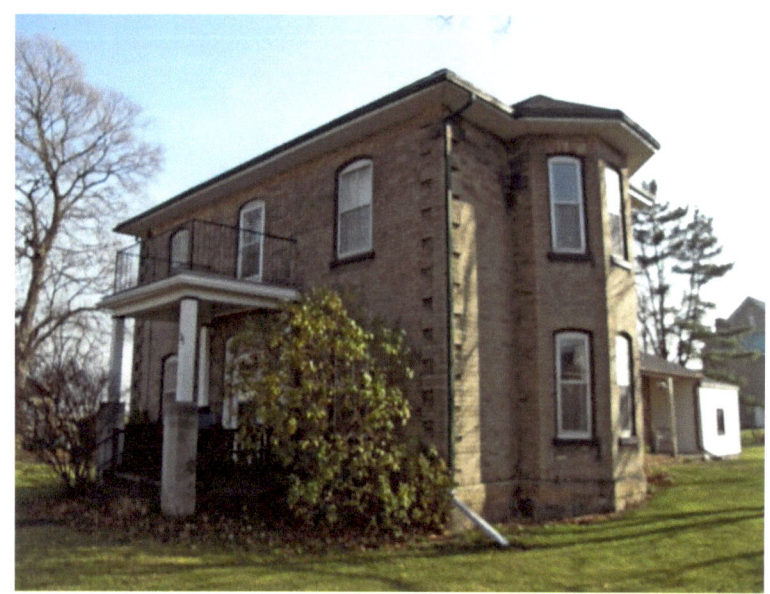

#23 – corner quoins, two-storey bay window, second floor balcony

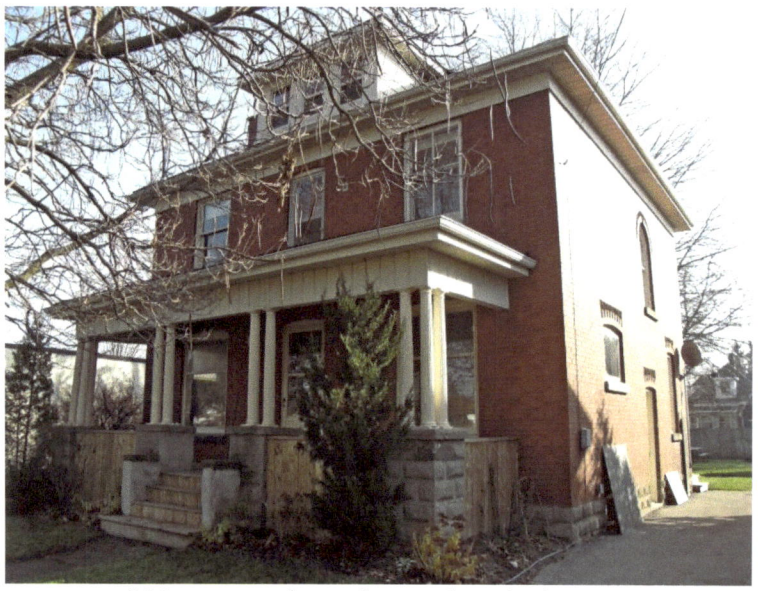

#20 - veranda on lower level, dormer

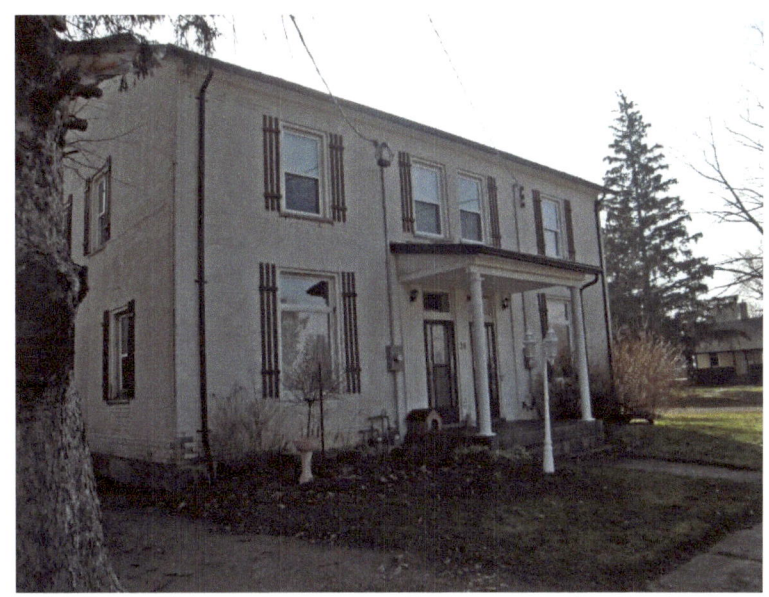

#28

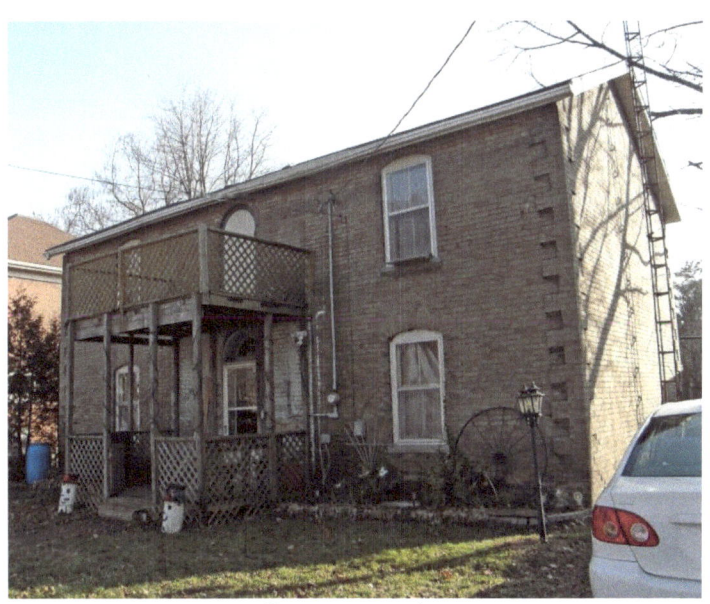

Corner quoins

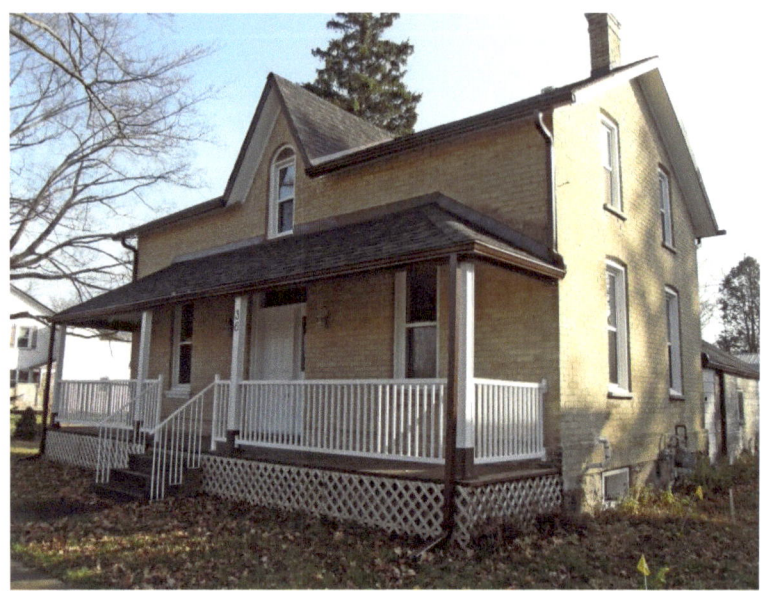

#36 – Gothic Revival Regency Cottage with small center arch

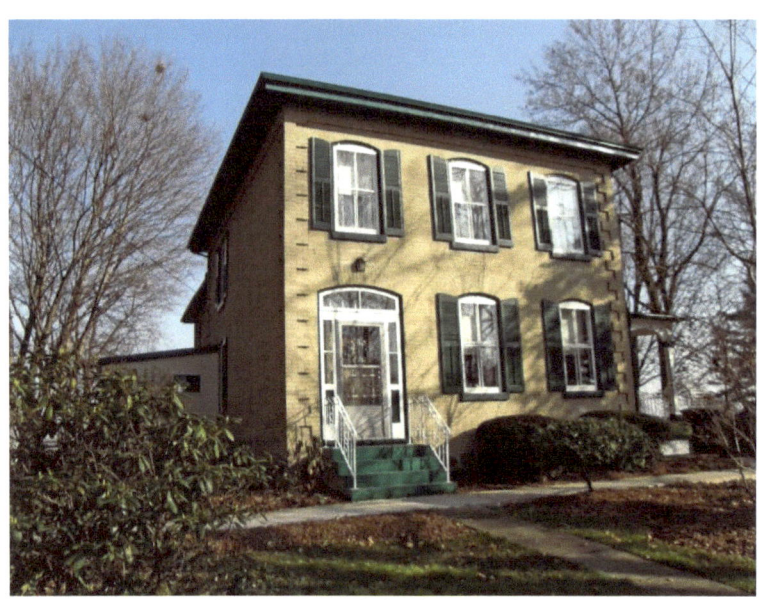

Corner quoins, shutters, sidelights and transom windows

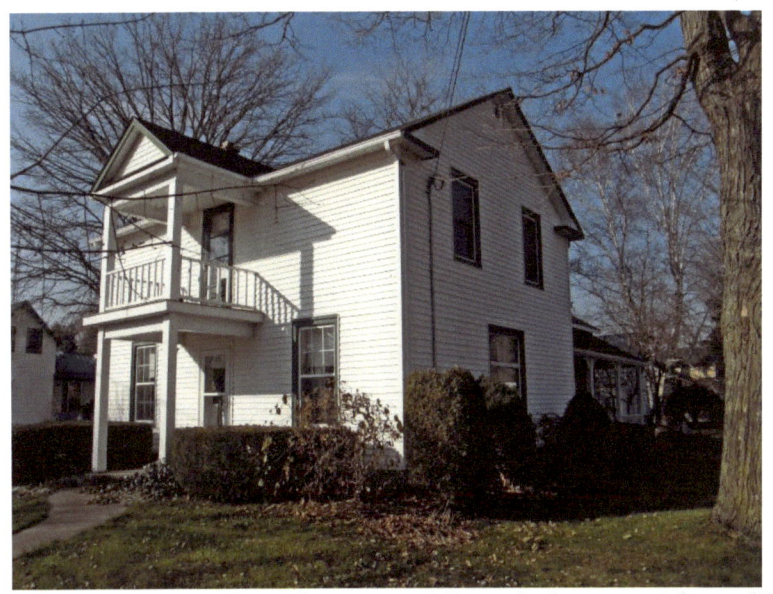

Cornice return on end gable, second floor balcony with pediment

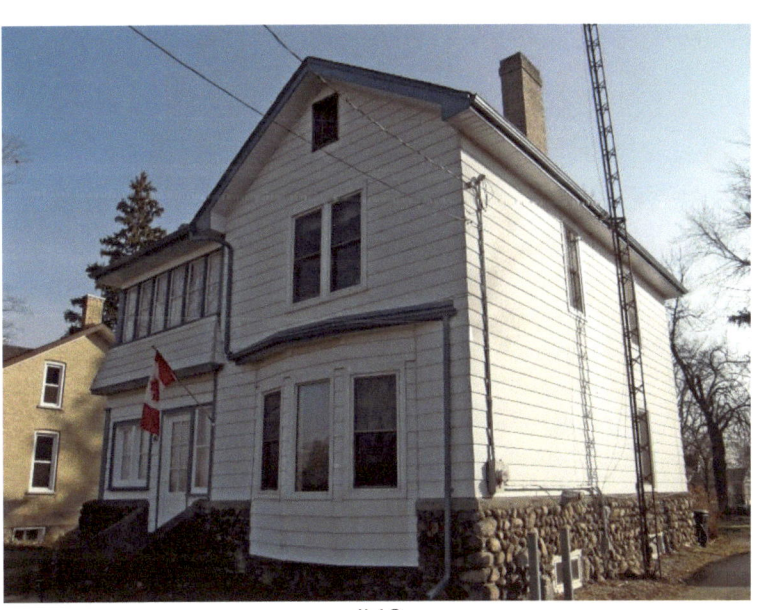

#40

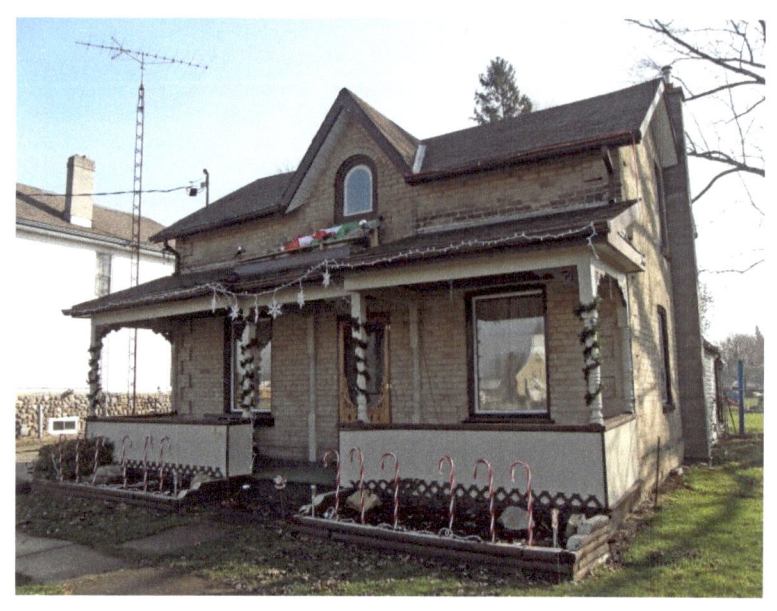

Both are Gothic Revival Regency Cottages

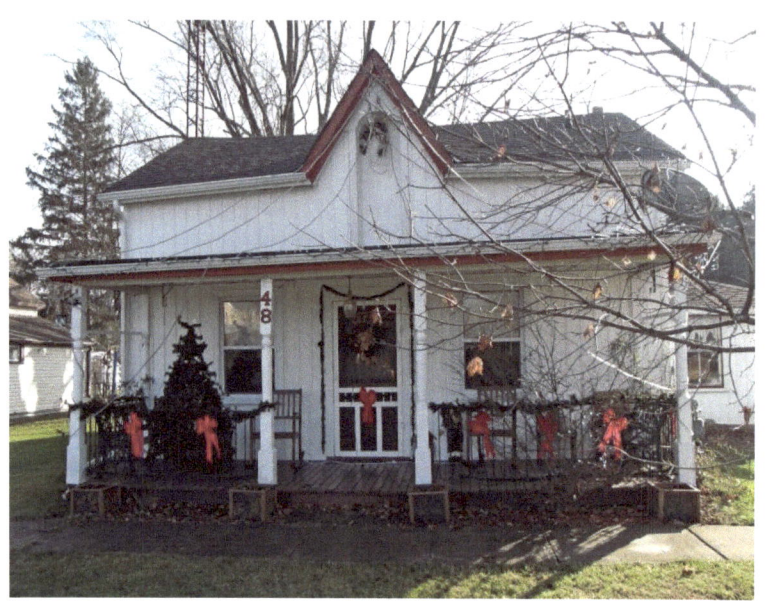

#48

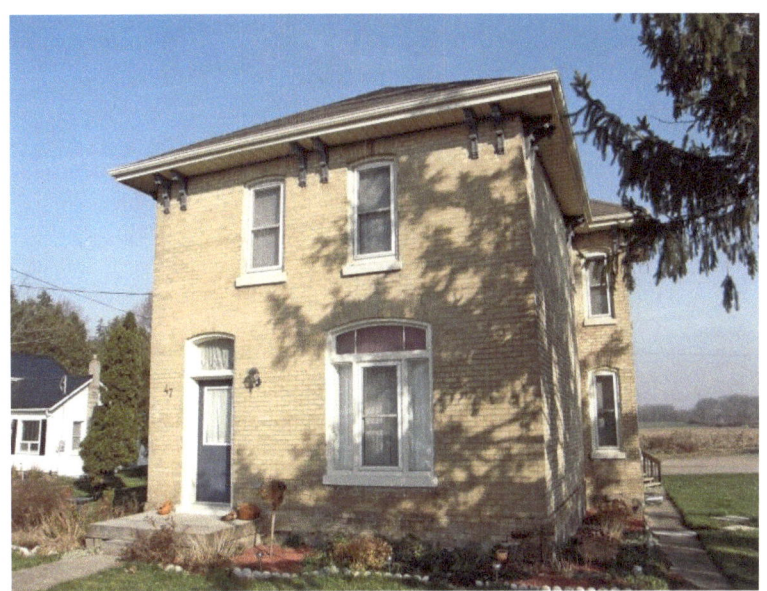

#47 – yellow brick with brick foundation, hip roof, paired cornice brackets

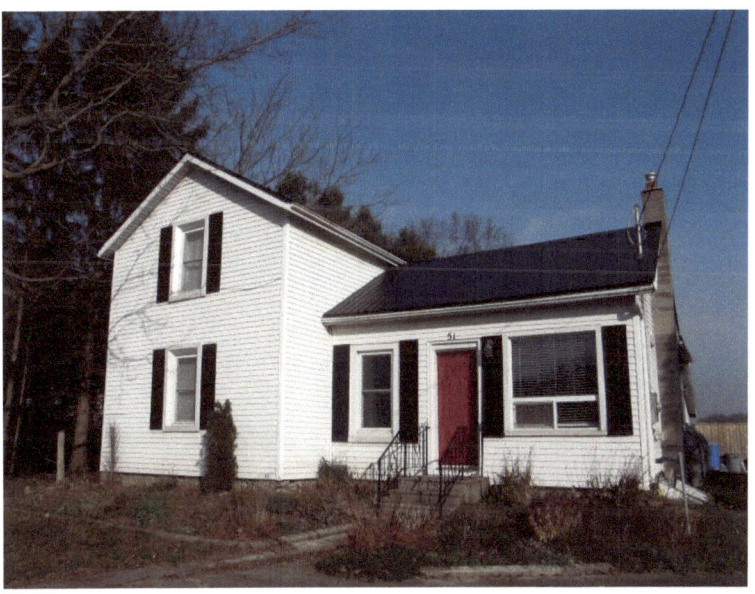

#51

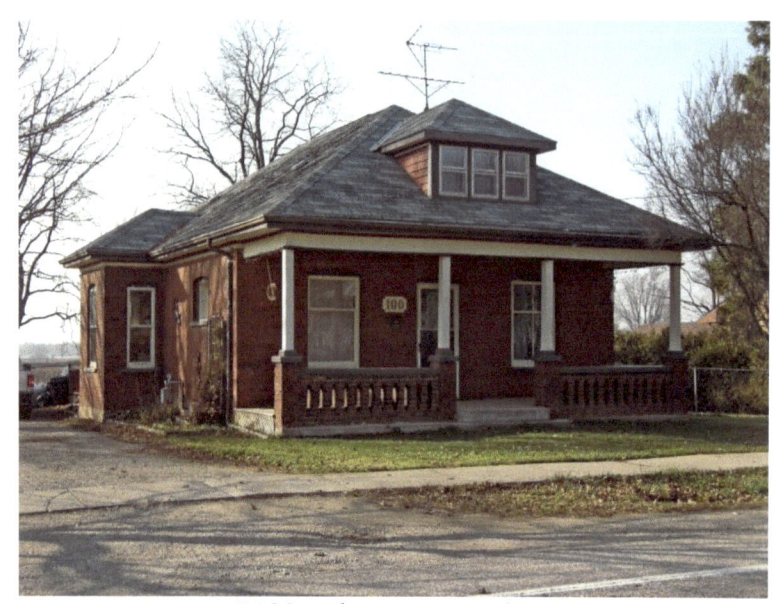

#100 – dormer window

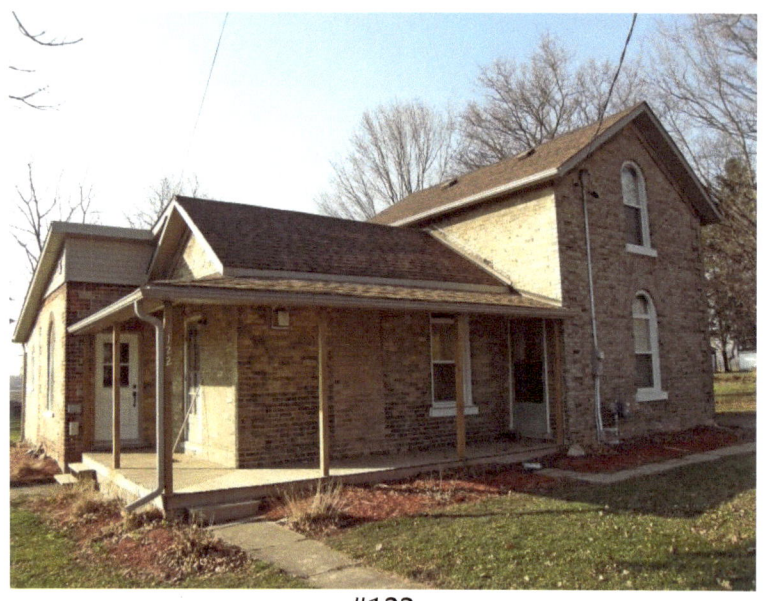

#122

Etonia

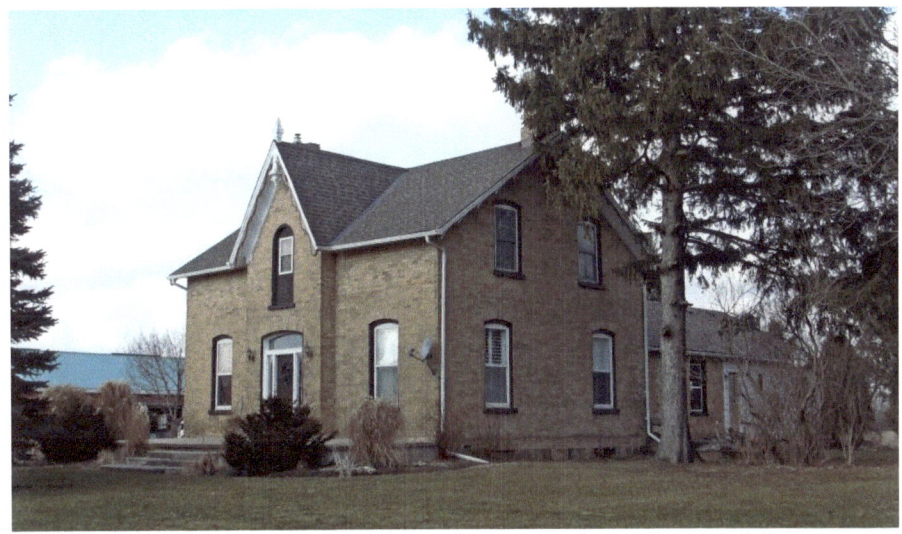

Gothic Revival - finial on the verge board on gable

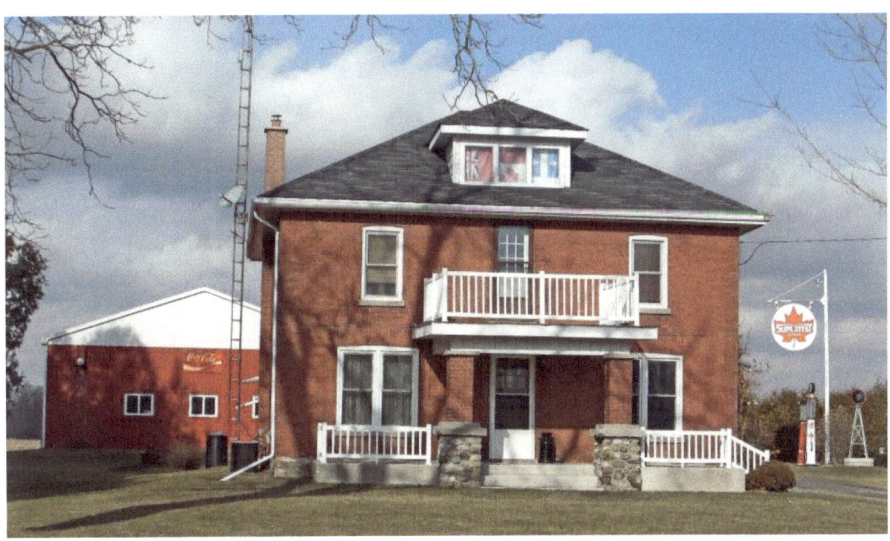

Italianate, dormer in attic, second floor balcony

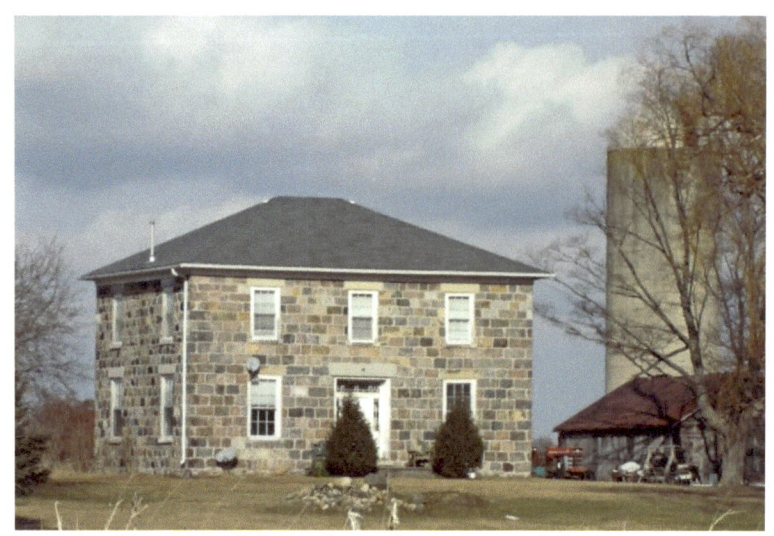

Italianate – hipped roof, stone architecture

Gobles

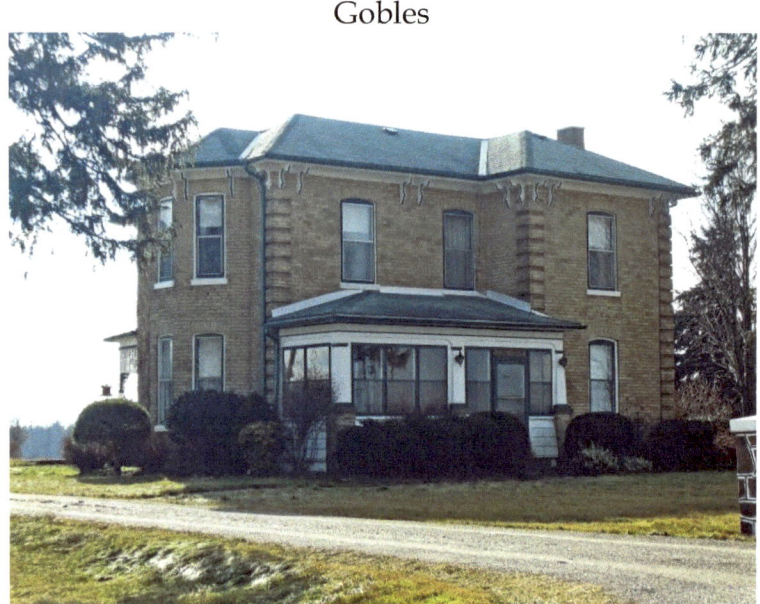

Richwood

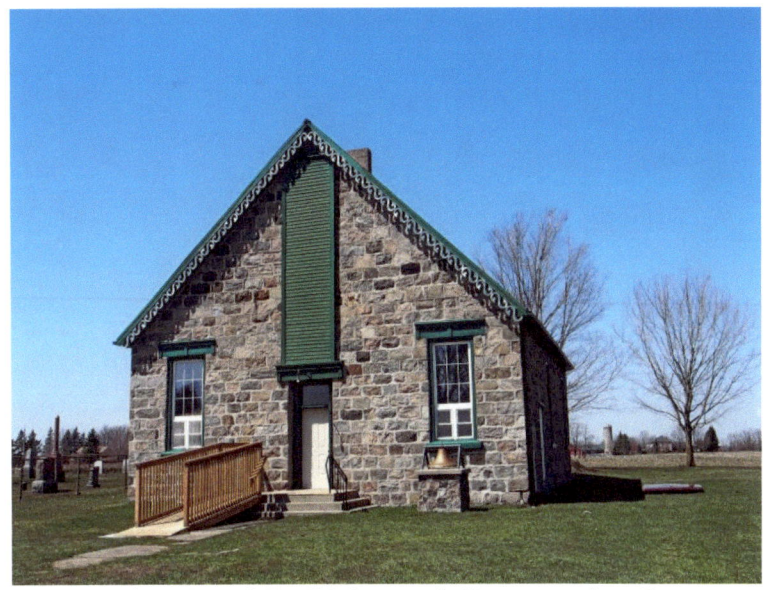

767415 Township Road 5 - Richwood Community Centre - stone

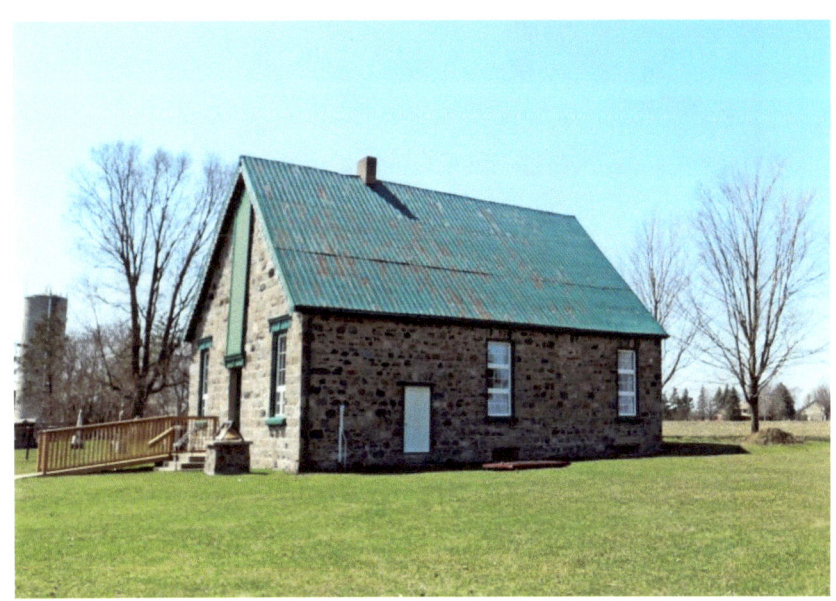

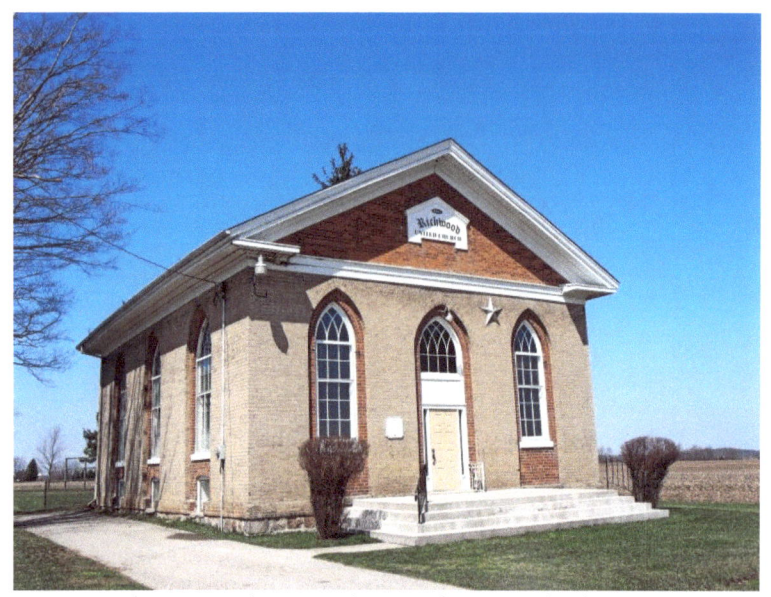

767417 Township Road 5 - Richwood United Church – 1861 – Gothic – lancet windows, cornice return on gable

Wolverton

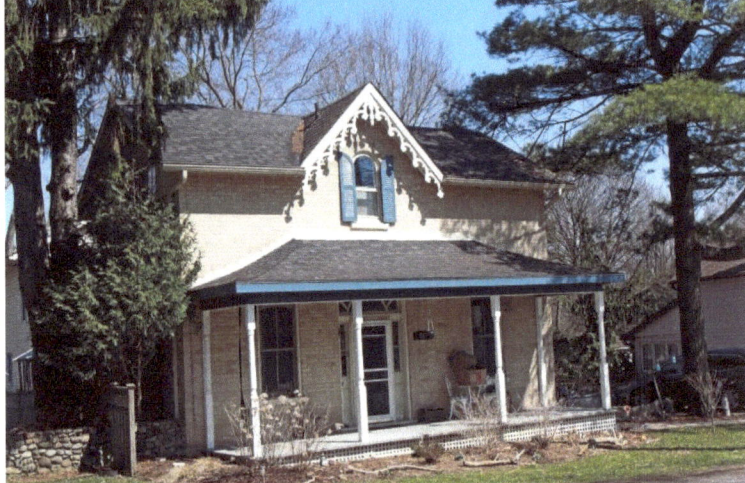

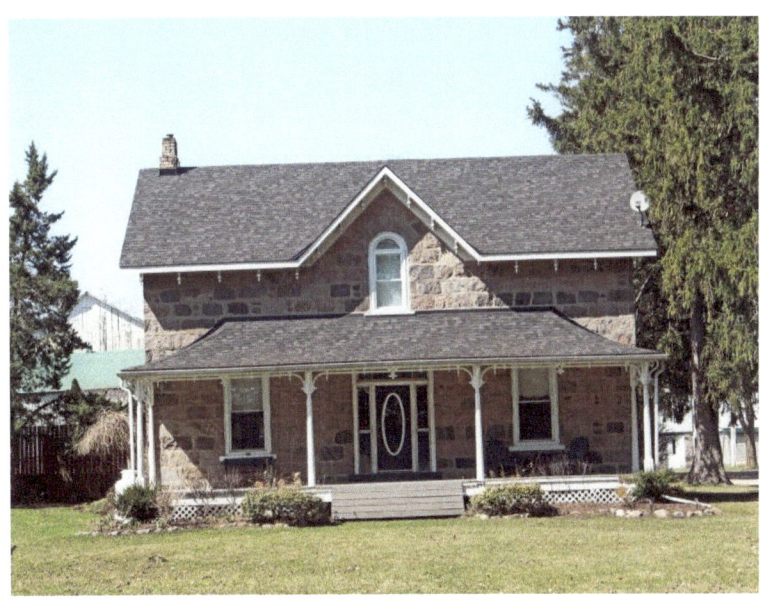

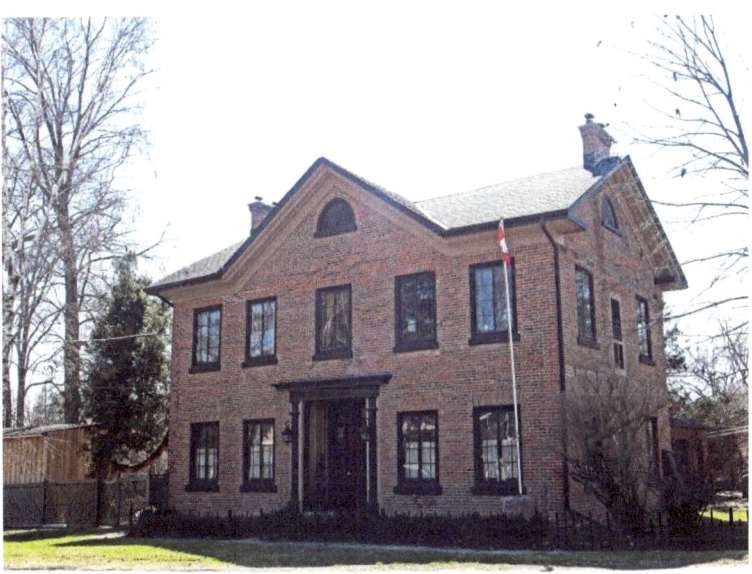

About 1855, Enos Wolverton built an impressive new three storey family home with a cupola which came to be known as Wolverton Hall – Regency style

Washington

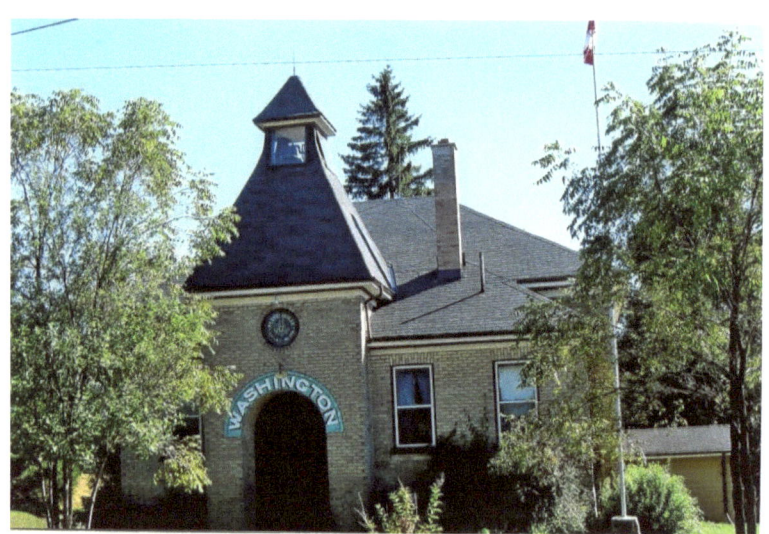

Cupola with bell

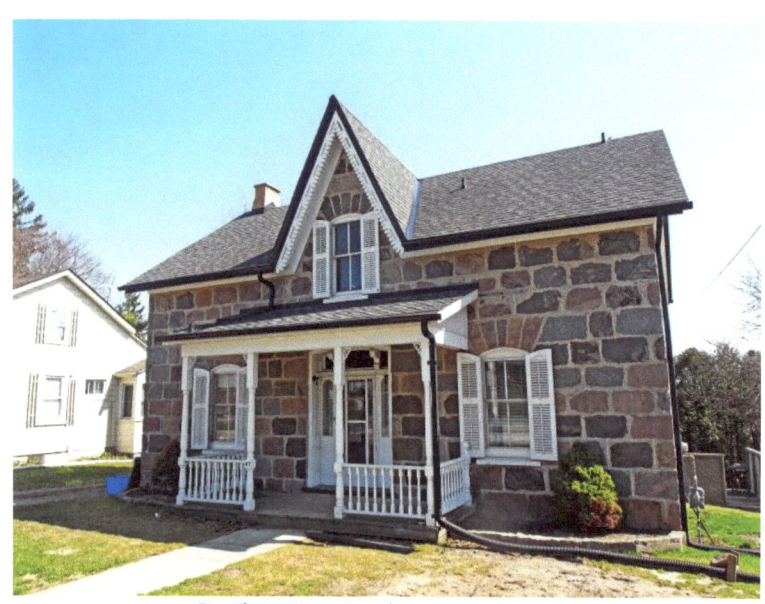

Gothic Revival stone cottage

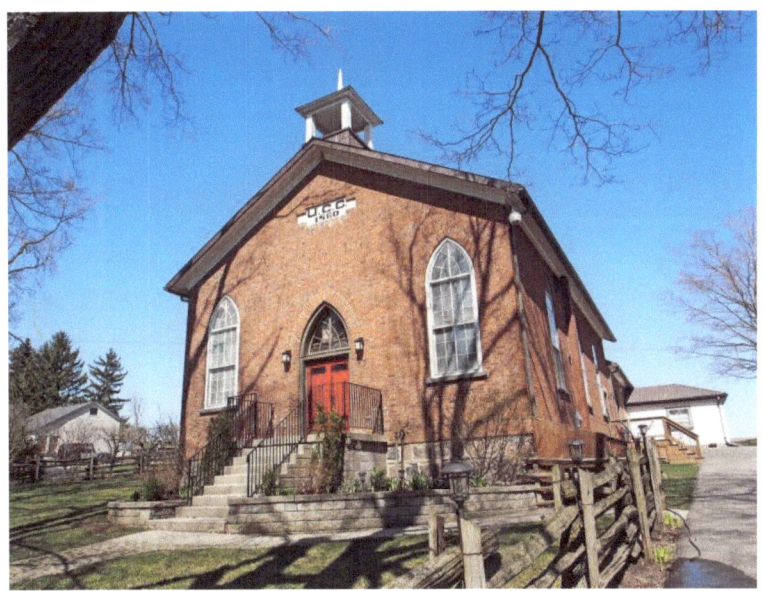

23 Washington Road North - Washington United Church – 1860

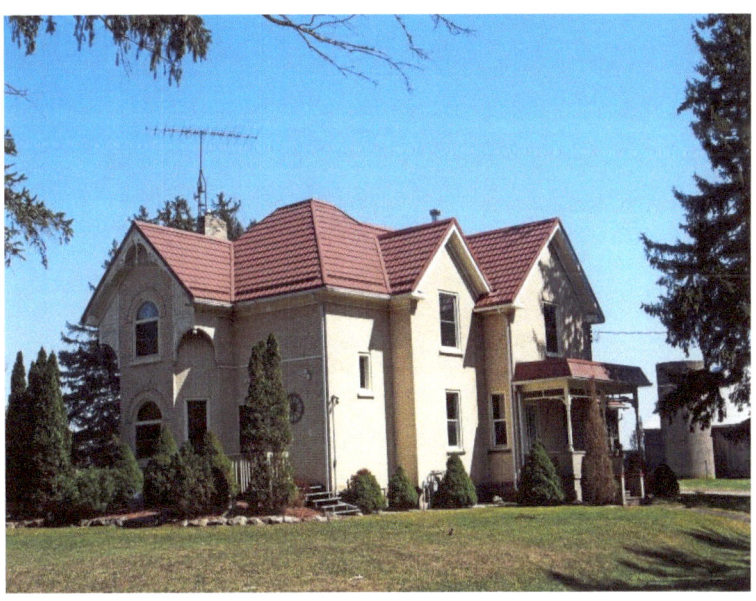

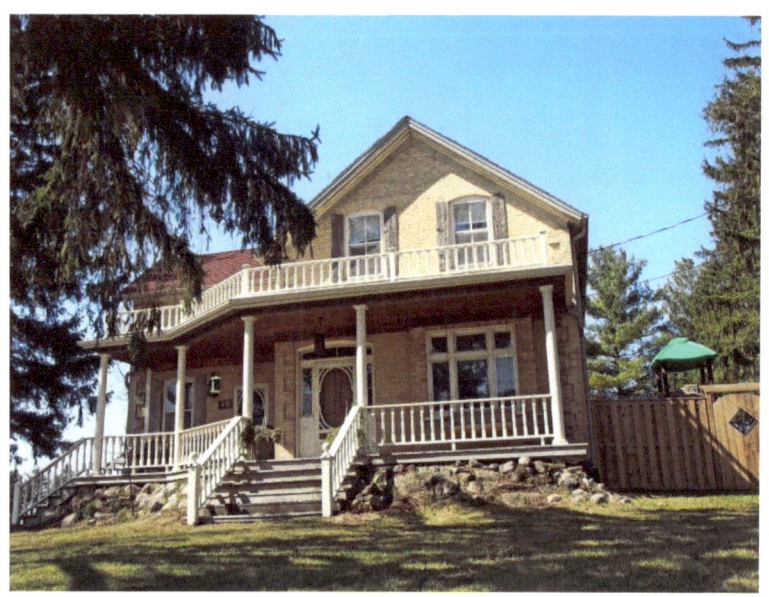

#48

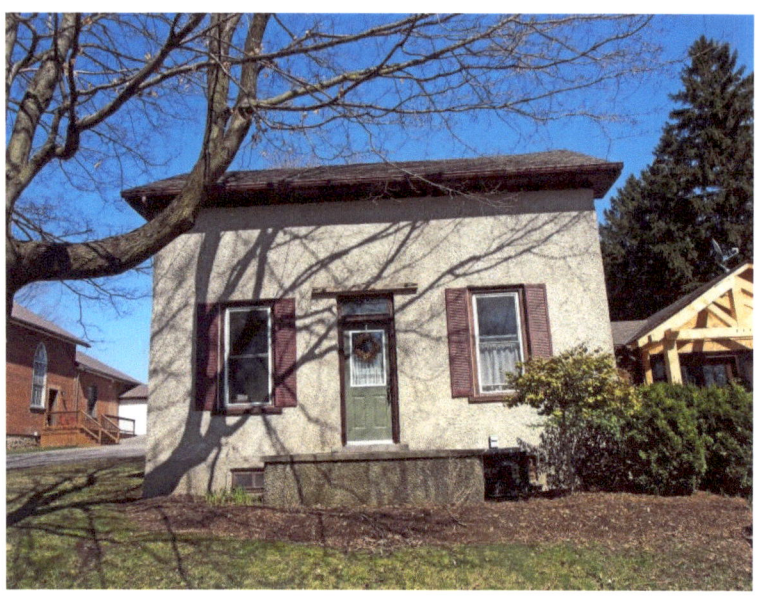

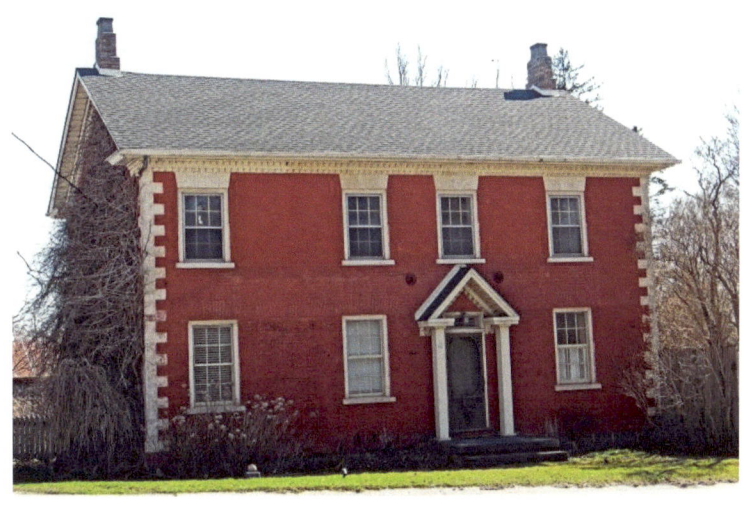

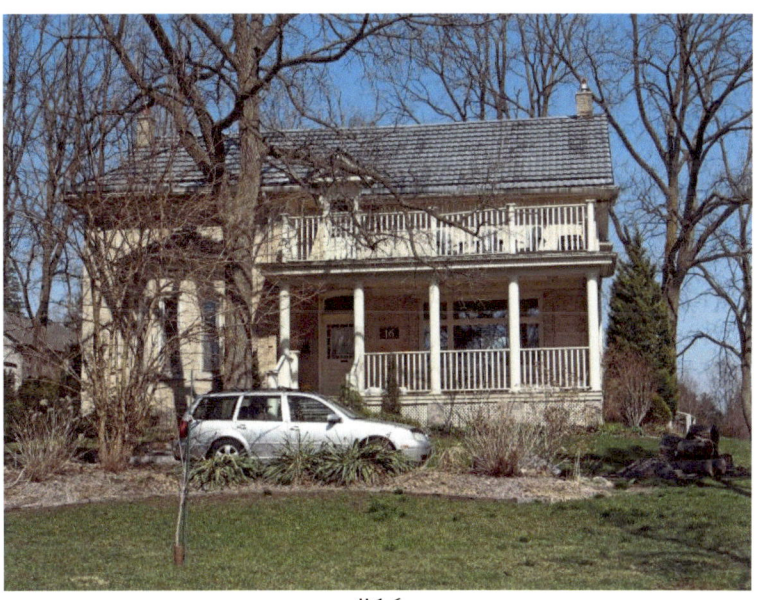

#16

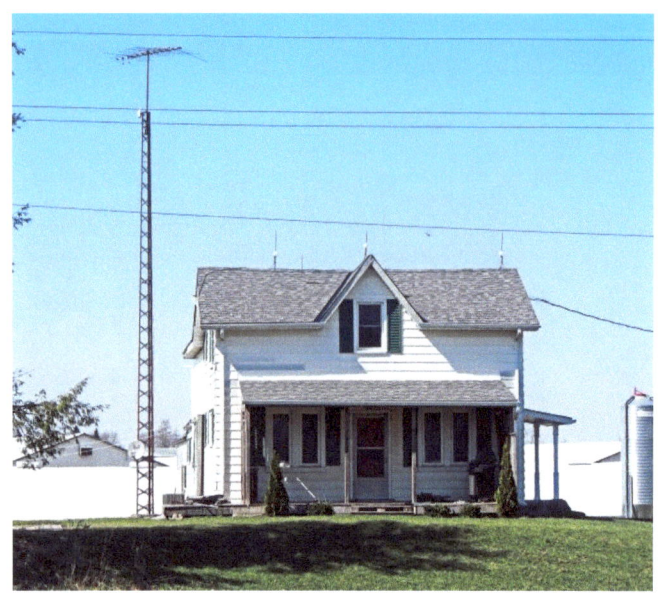

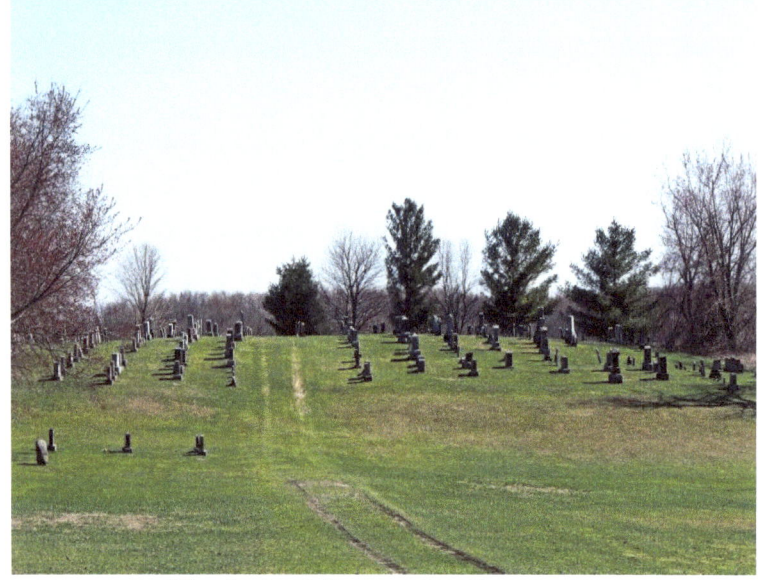

Blenheim Mennonite Cemetery

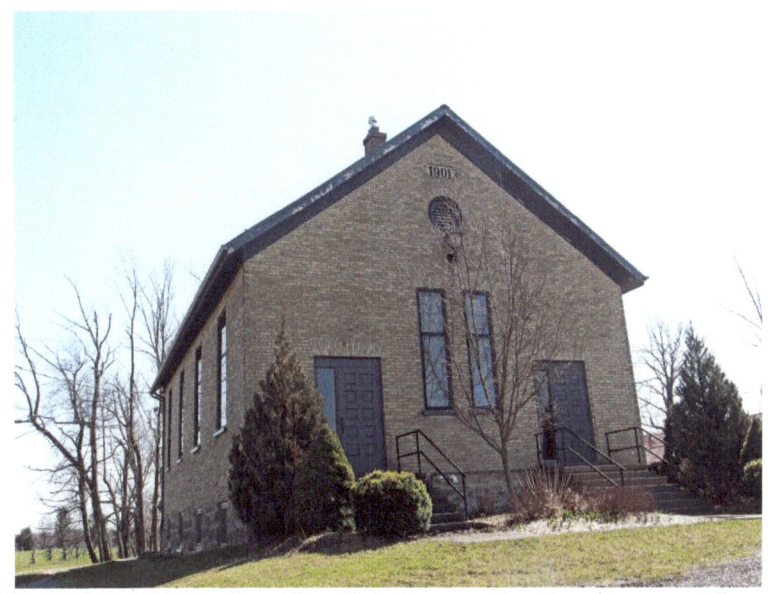

967244 Oxford-Waterloo Road -Mennonite Conference Church
Blenheim Retreat Centre

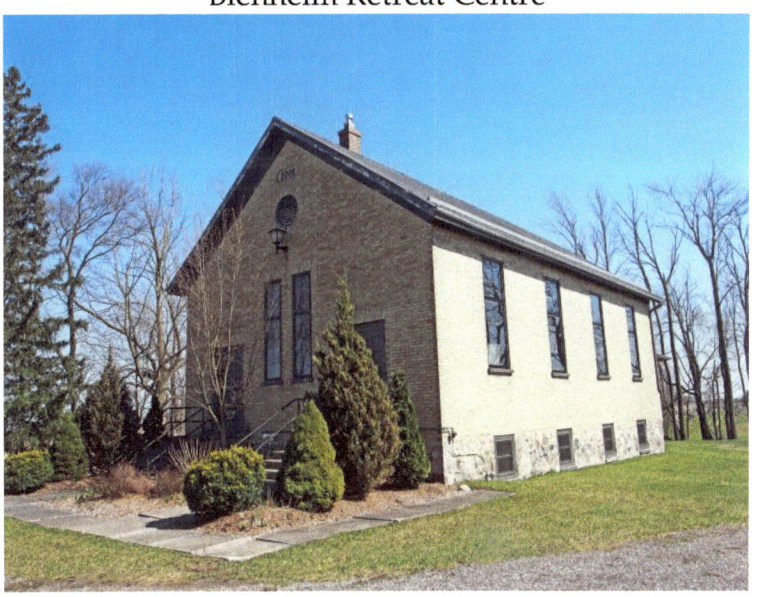

Plattsville

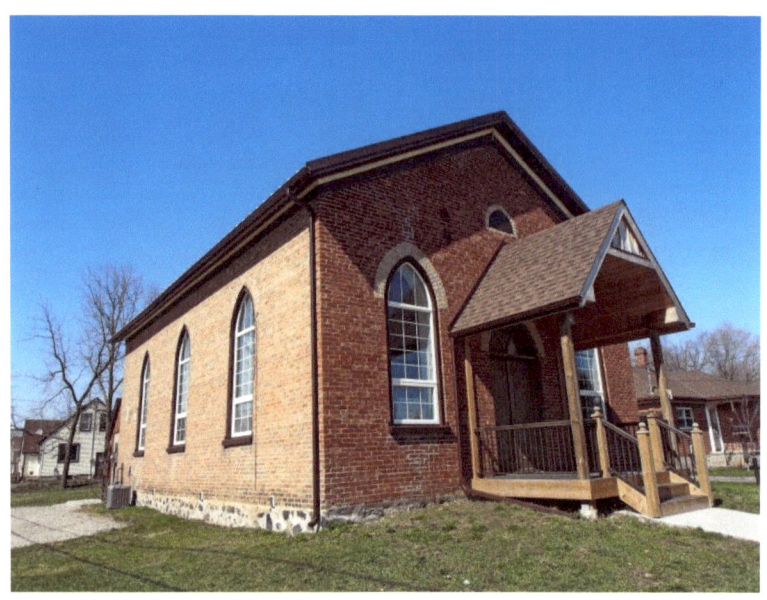

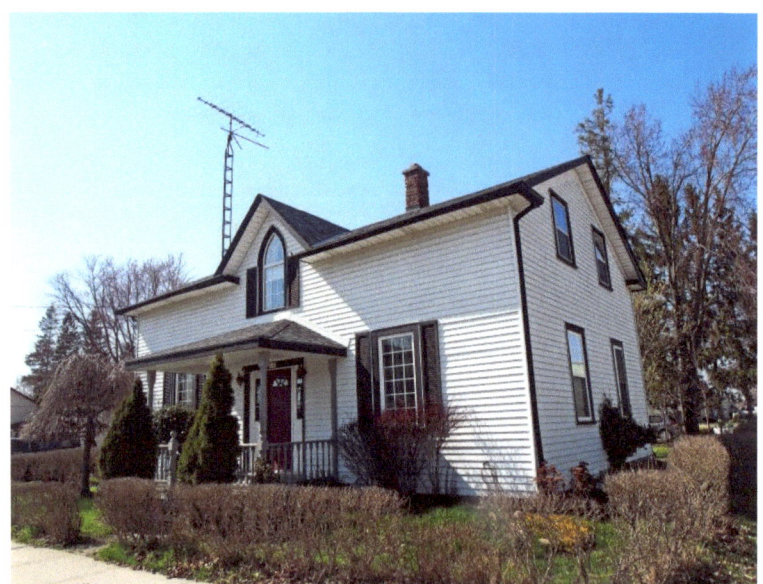

#56

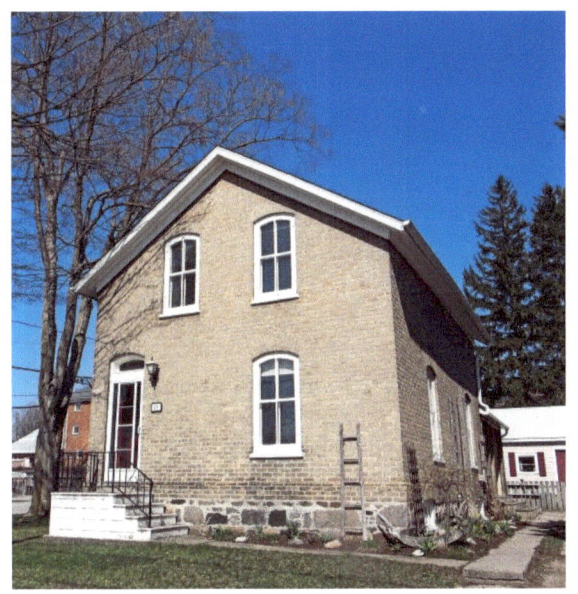

#19

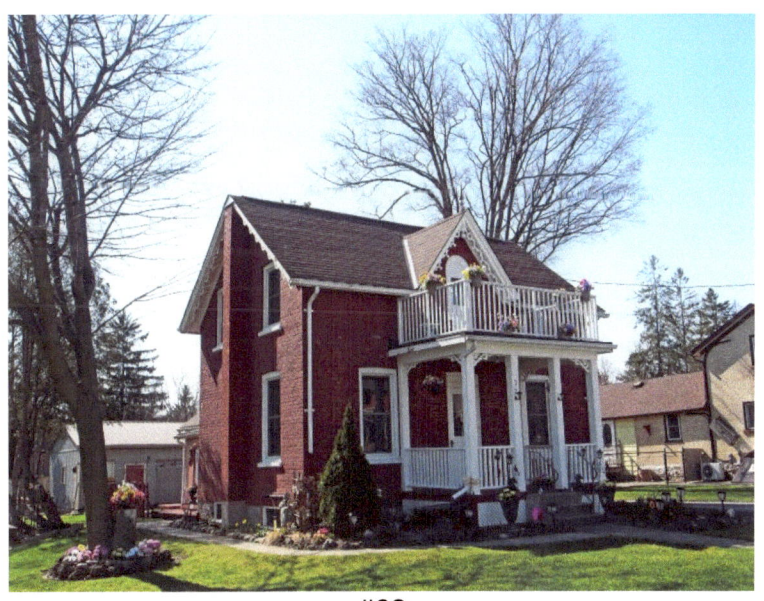

#32

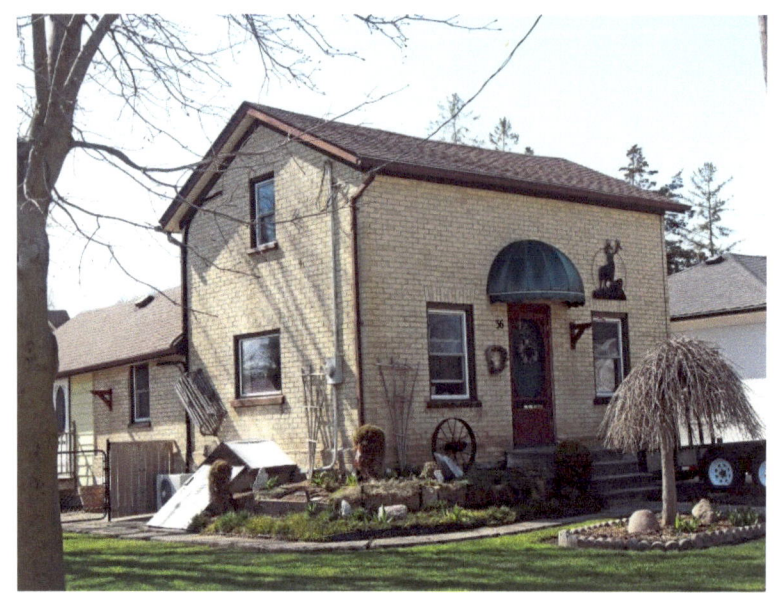

#36

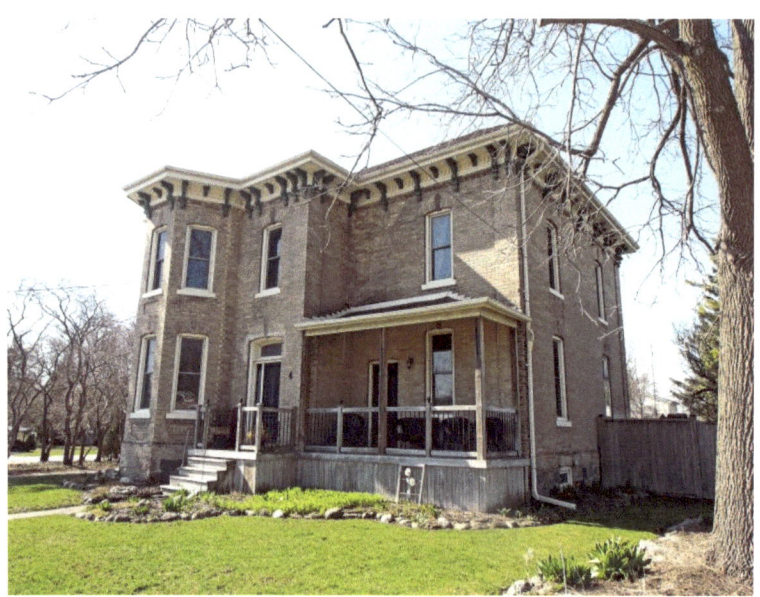

#4

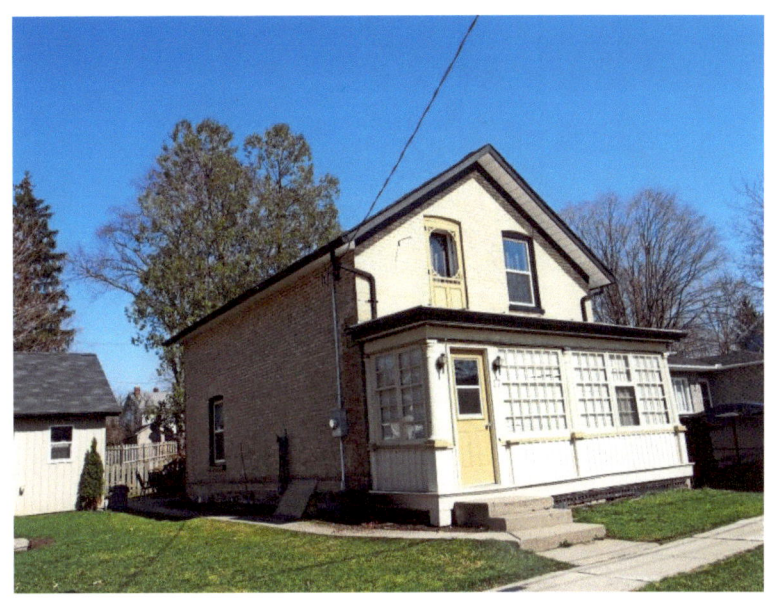

#17

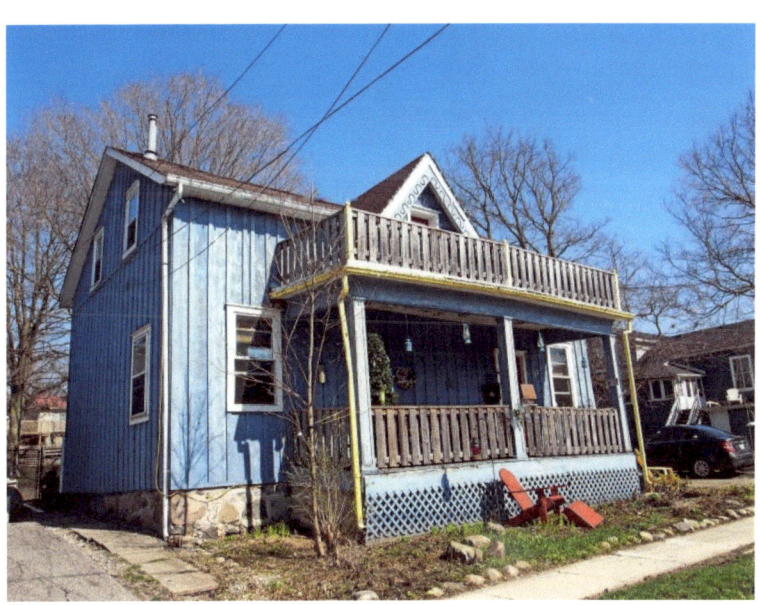

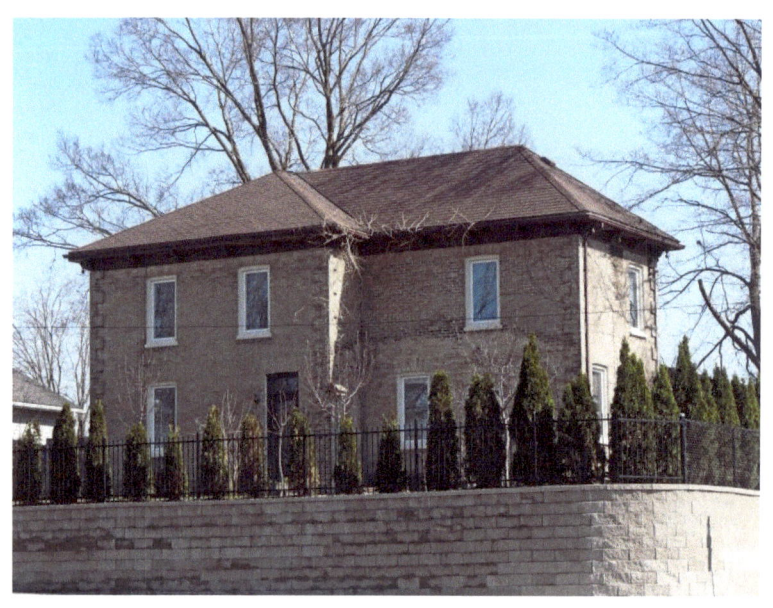

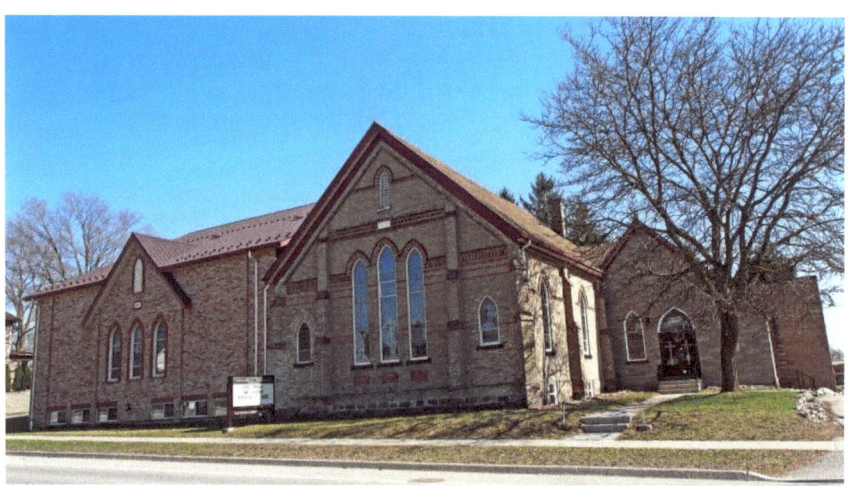

15 Albert Street East -Plattsville Evangelical Missionary Church

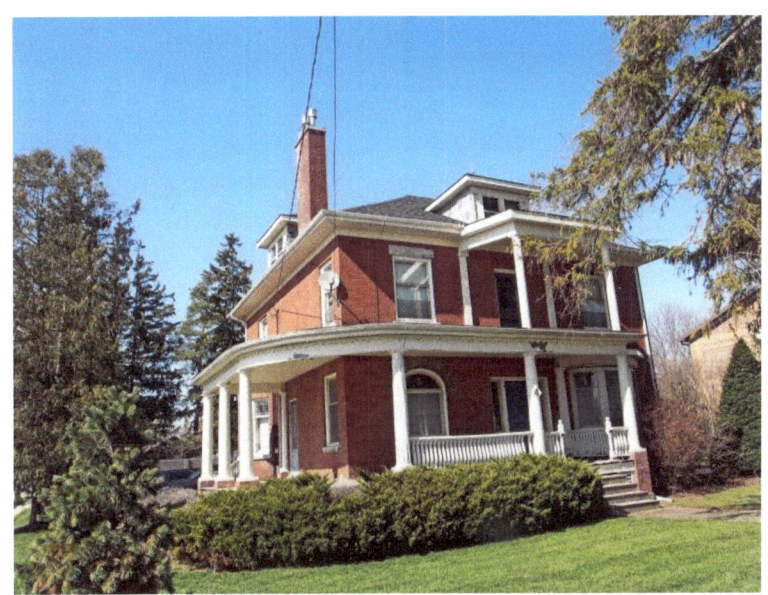

#4

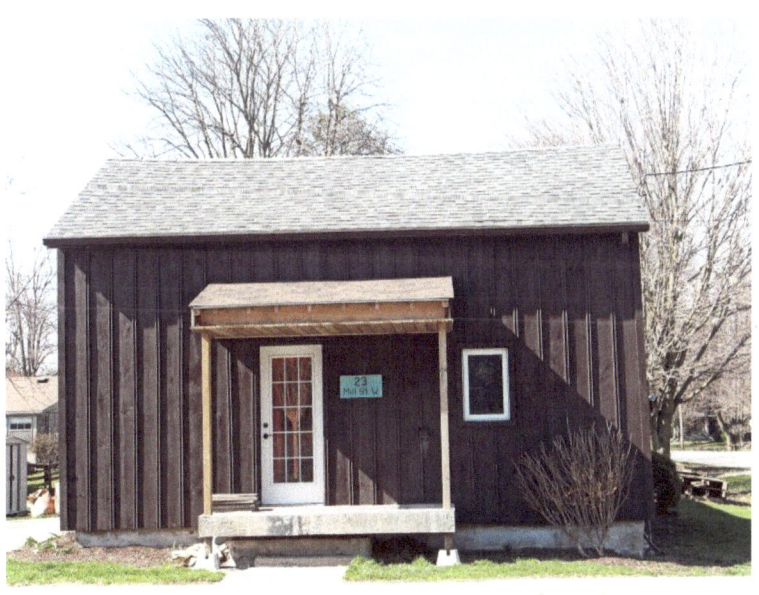

23 Mill Street West

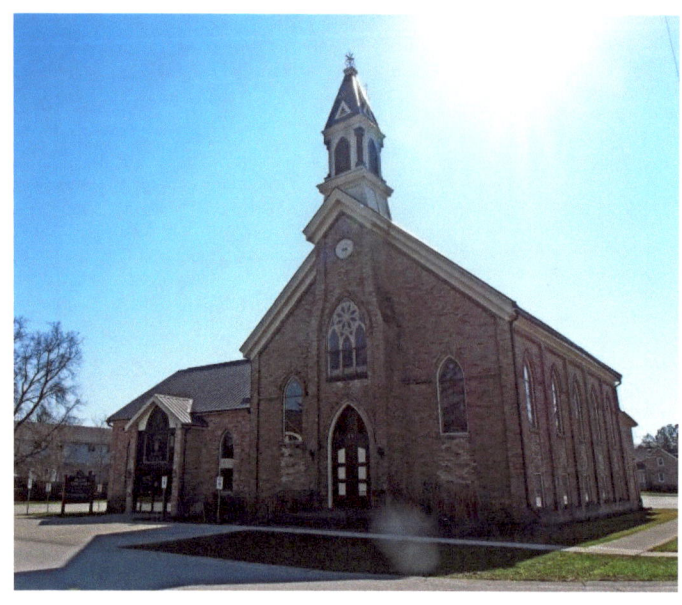

Peace United Church – Gothic – lancet windows, rose window, cupola

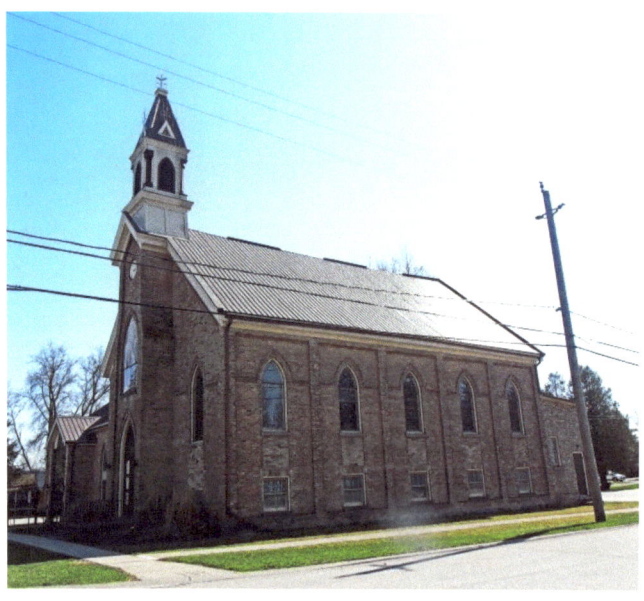

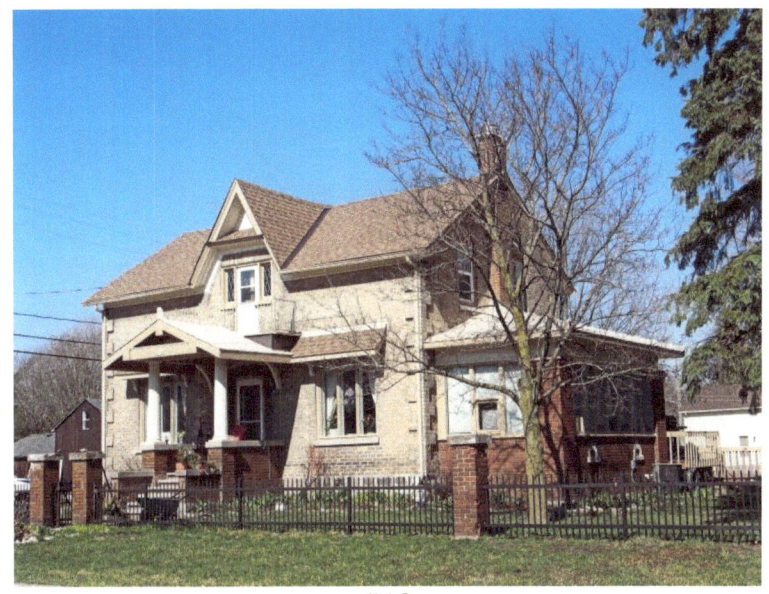

#19

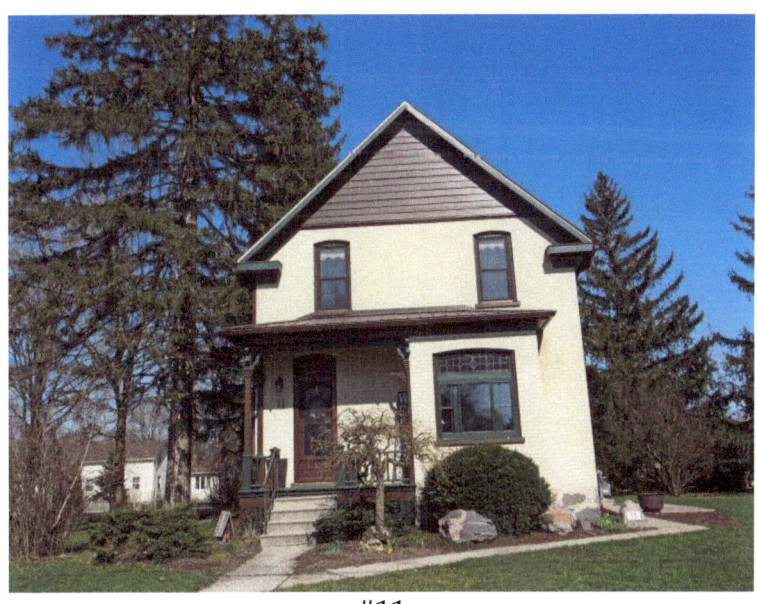

#11

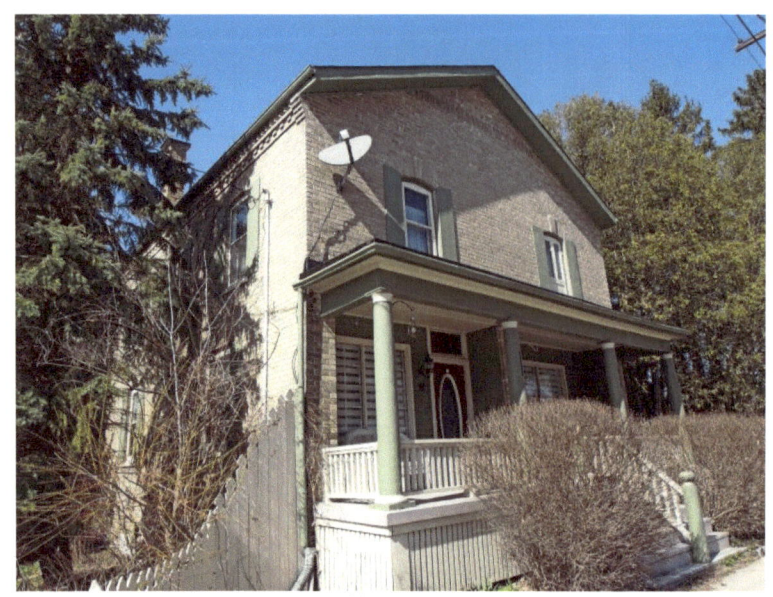

31 Albert Street

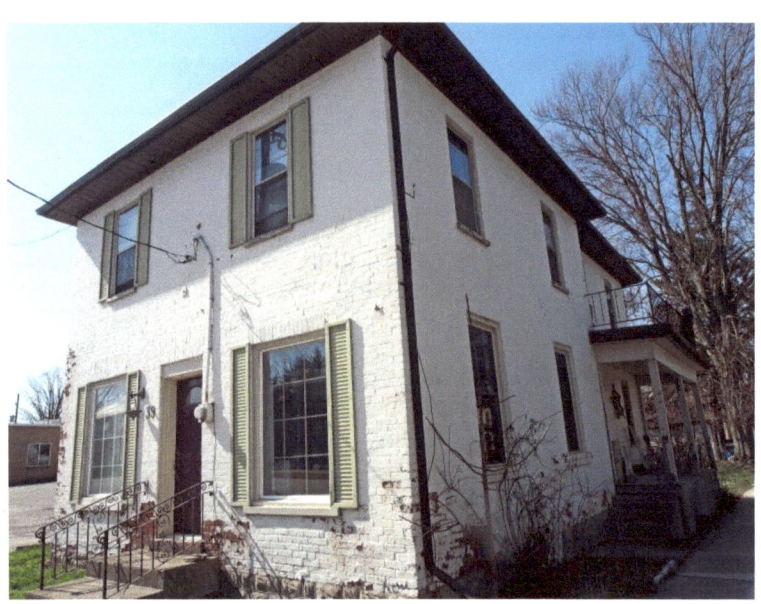

39 Albert Street

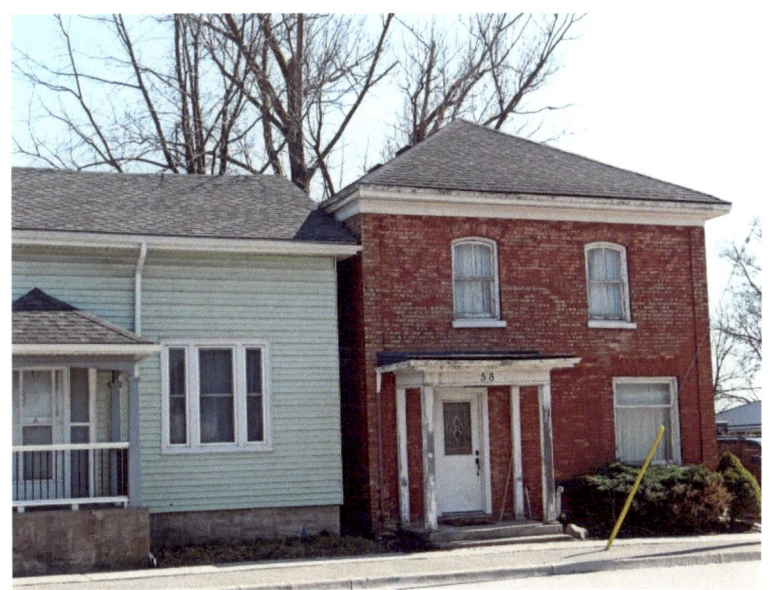

58 Albert Street

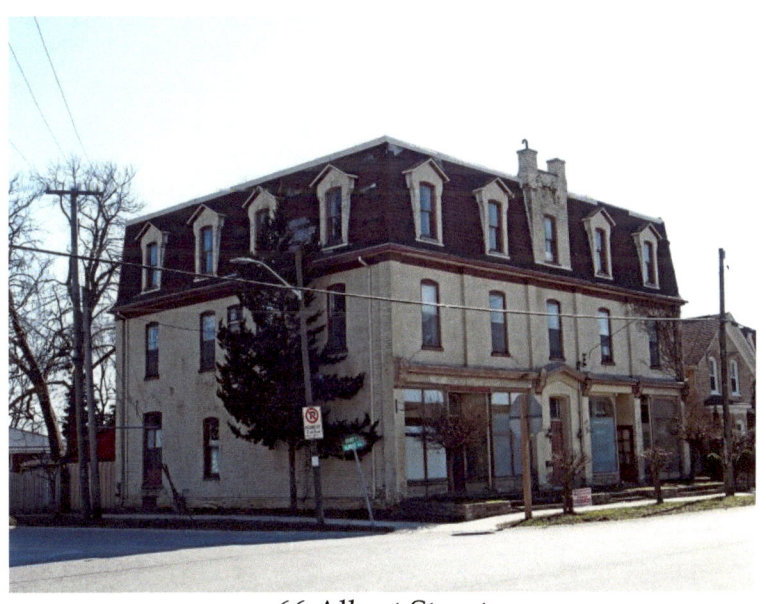

66 Albert Street

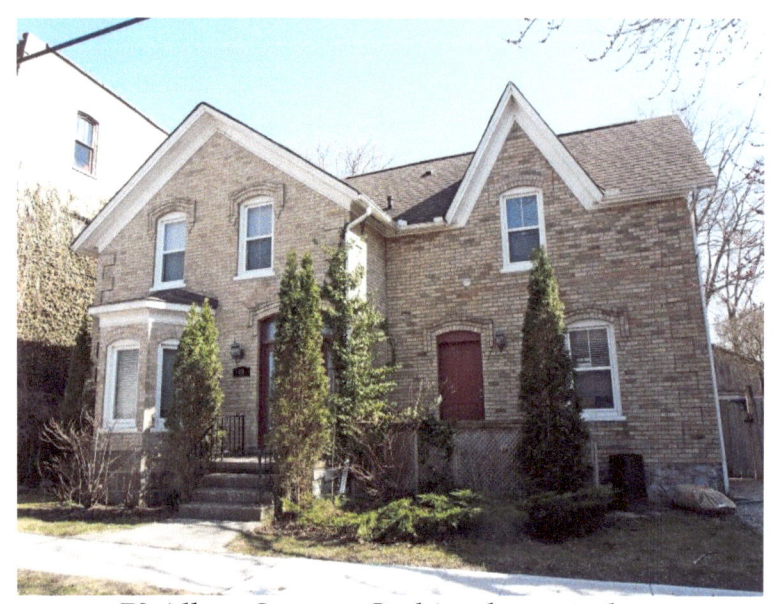

70 Albert Street – Gothic – bay window

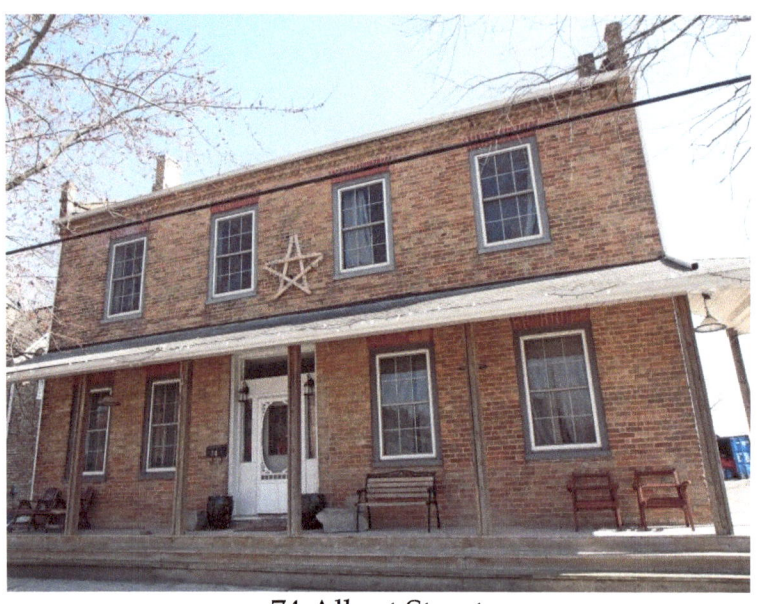

74 Albert Street

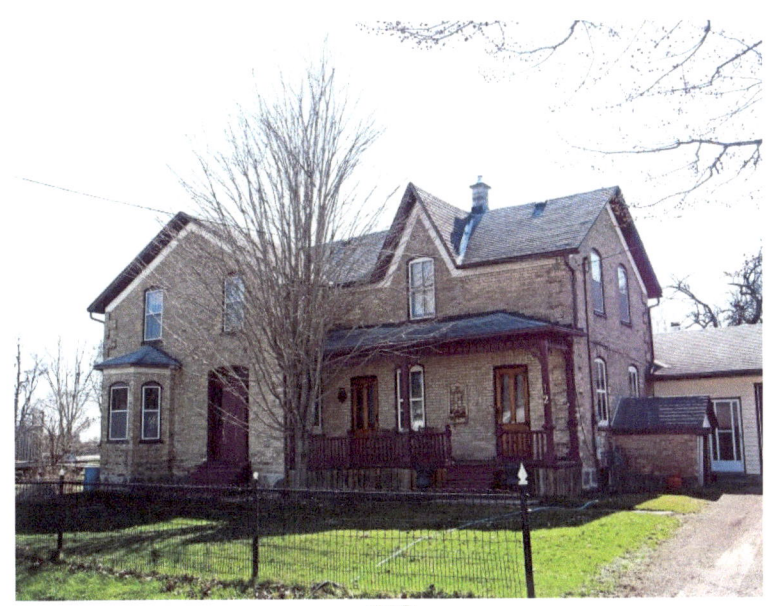

#12

Bright

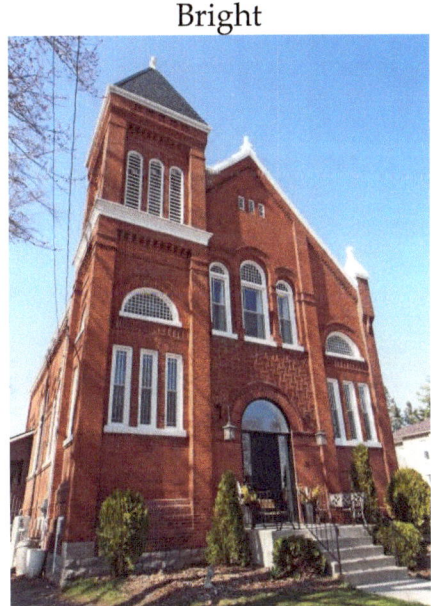

31 John Street West - Bright United Church

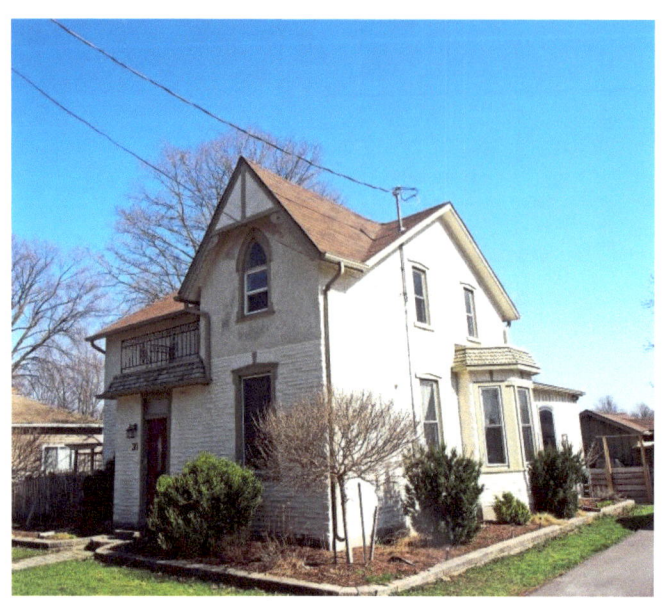

30 John Street West

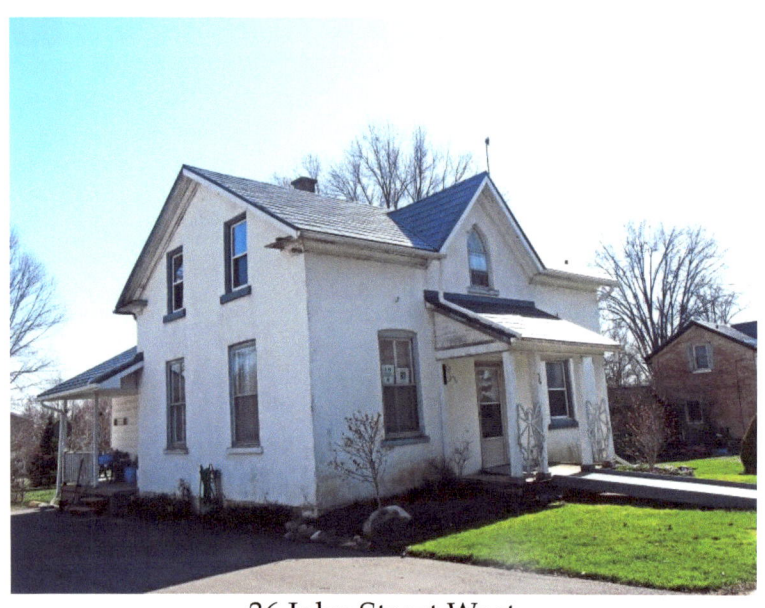

36 John Street West

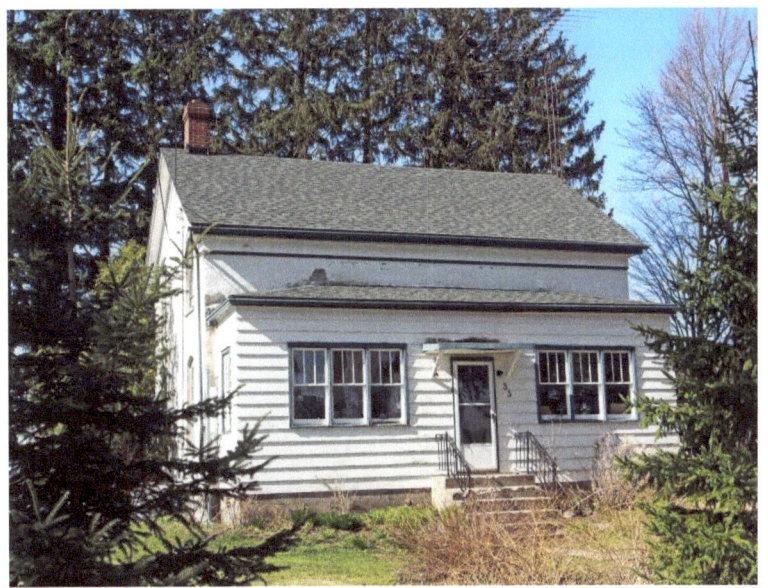

35 John Street West

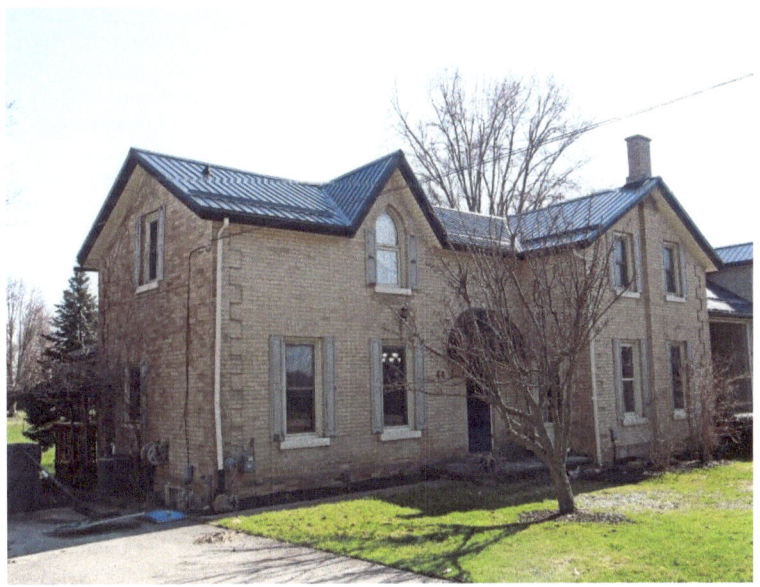

44 John Street West

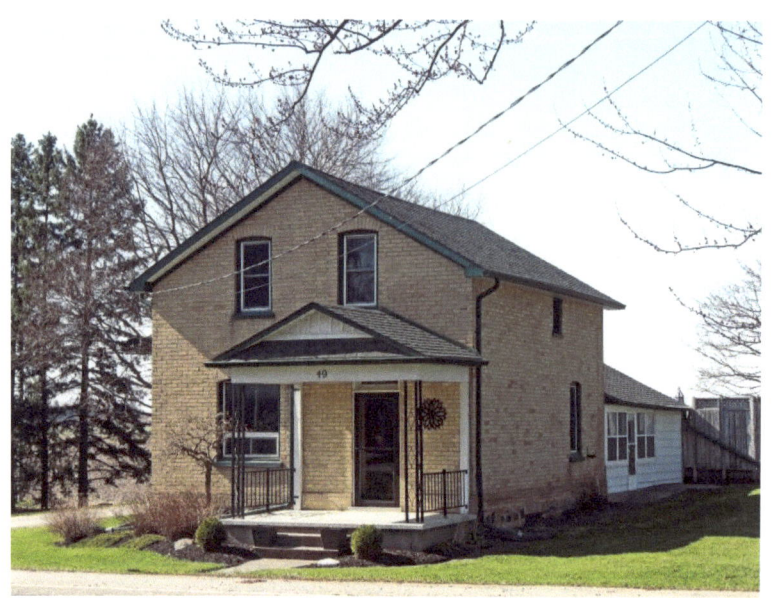

49 John Street West

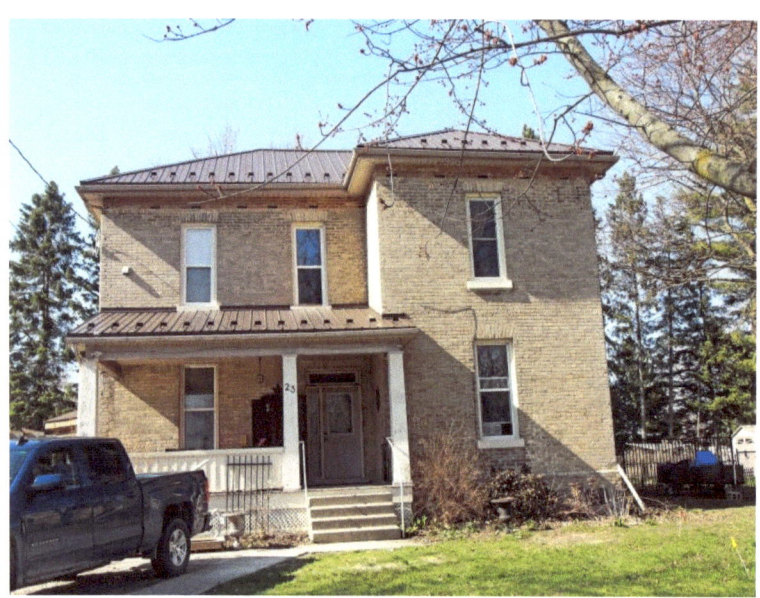

23 John Street West

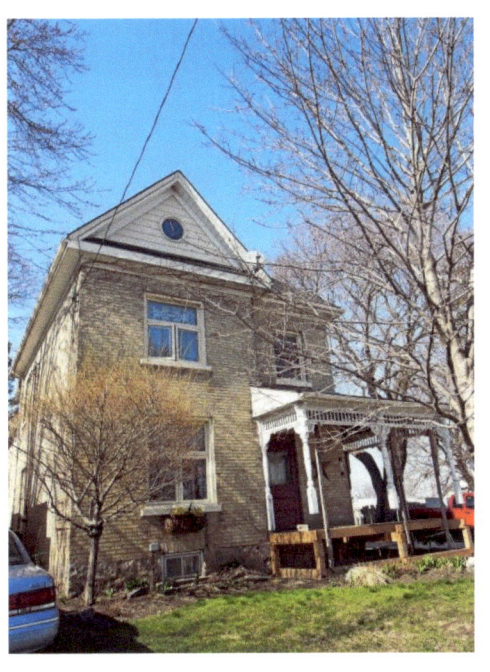

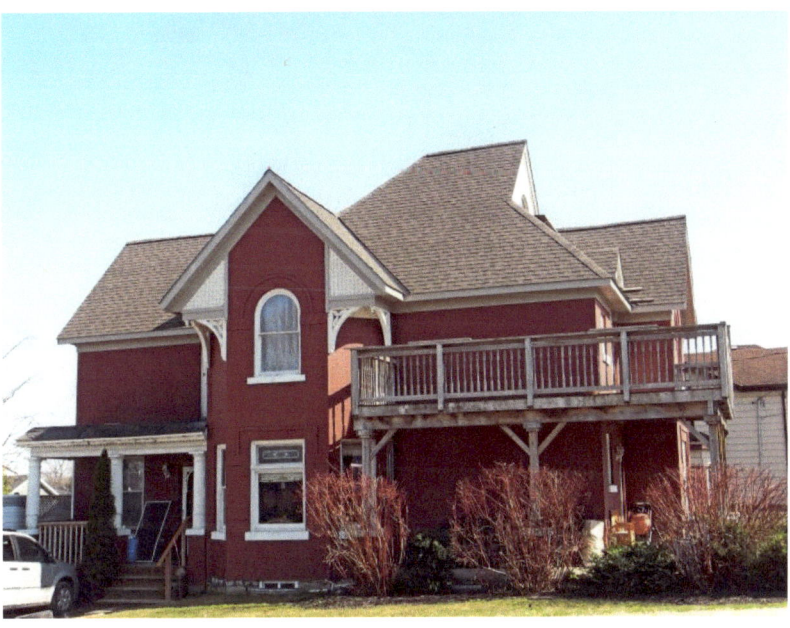

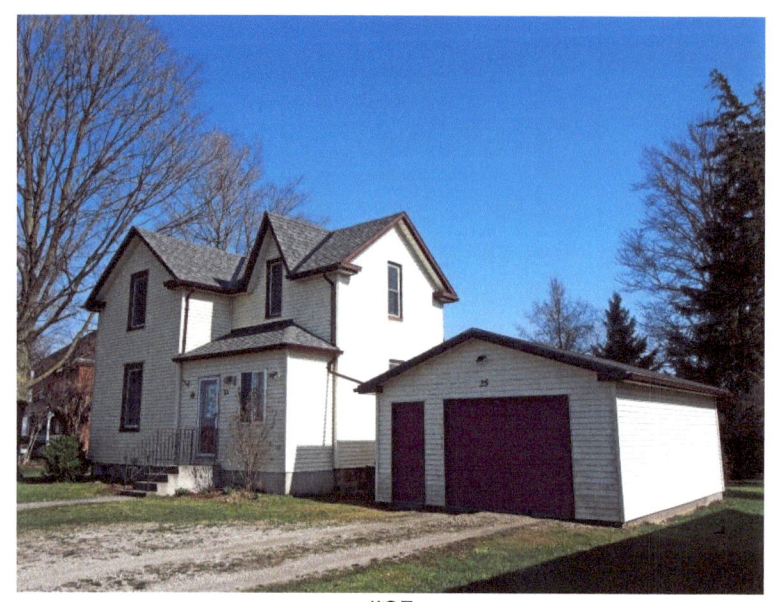

#25

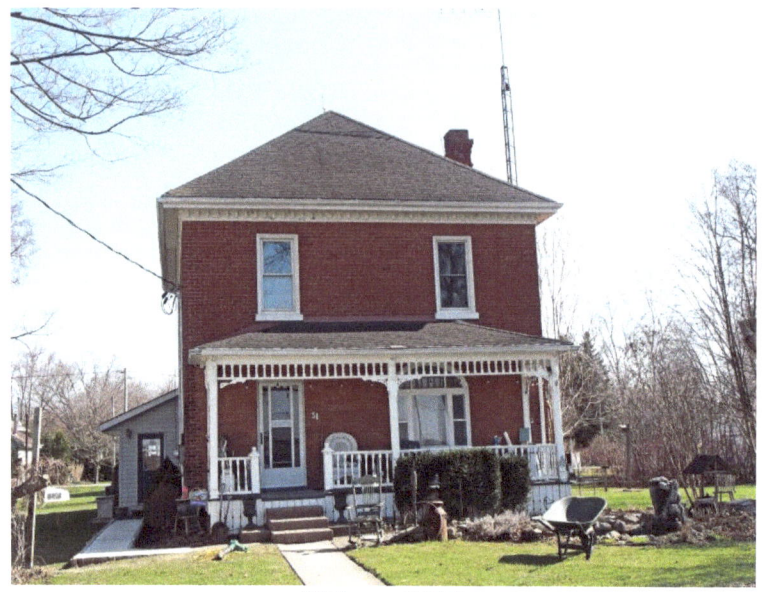

#31 - c. 1901

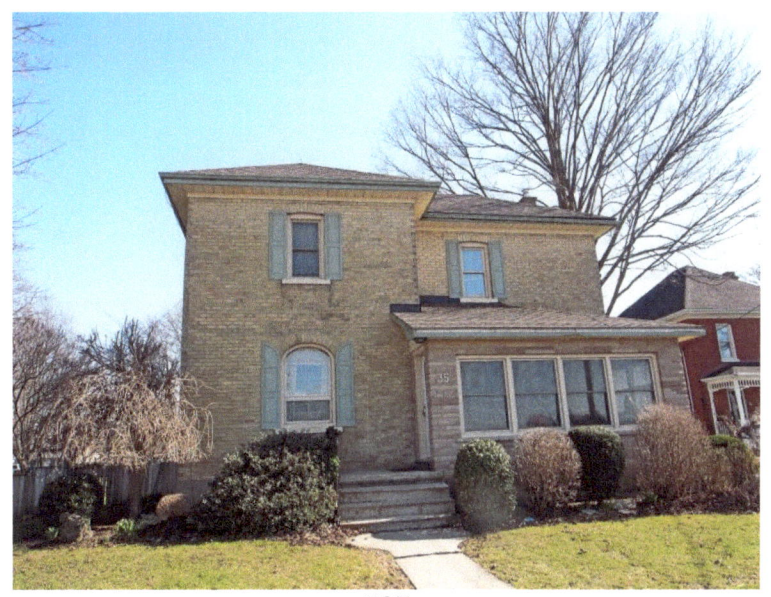

#35

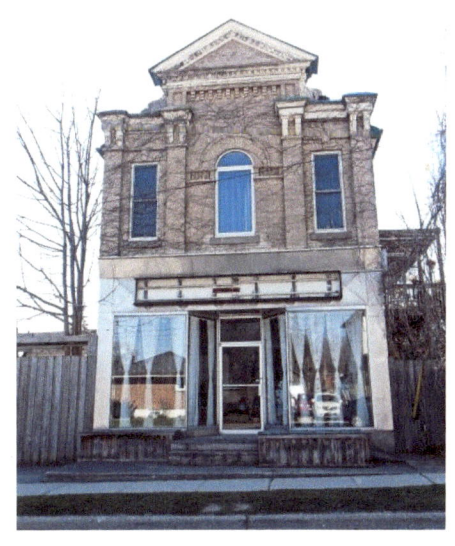

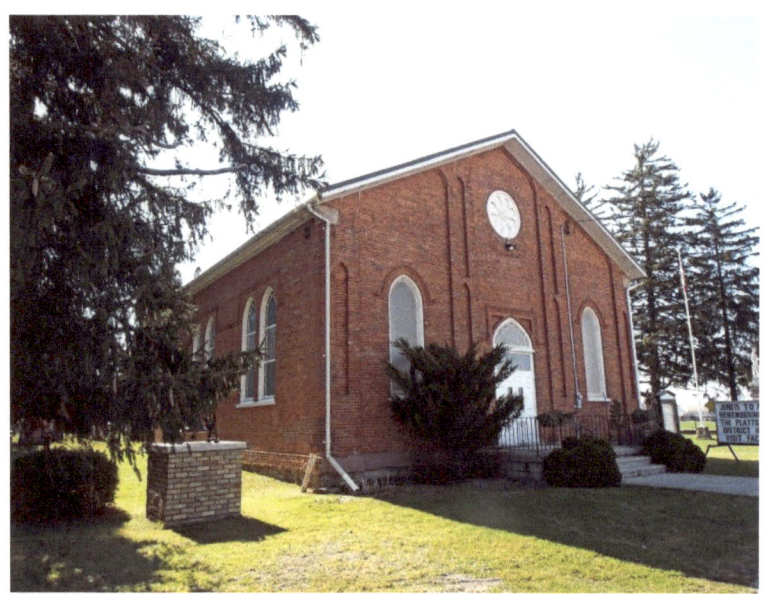

816661 Oxford Road 22 - Chesterfield United Church – 1855 – lancet windows, rose window

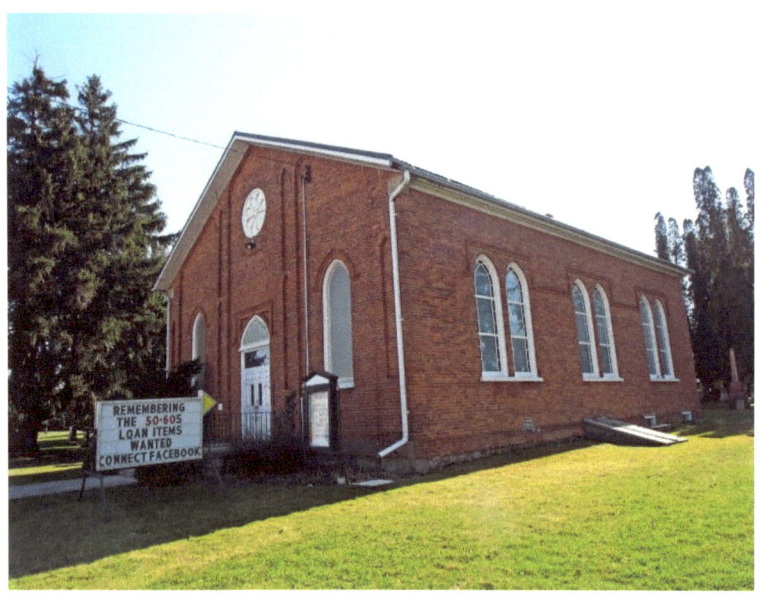

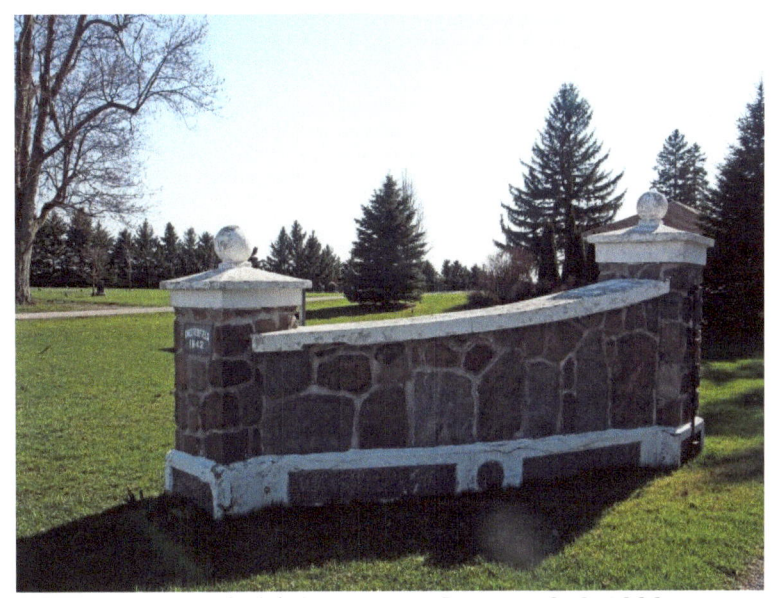

Chesterfield Cemetery Gate – 1842-1933

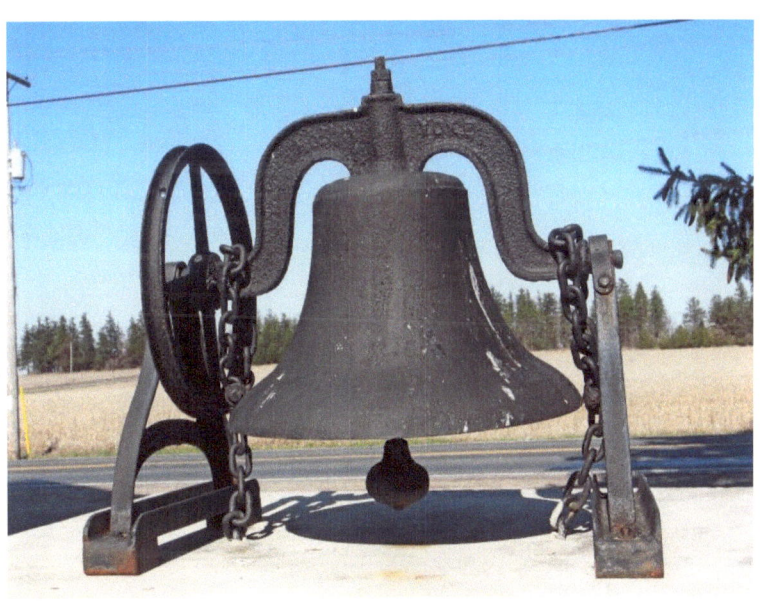

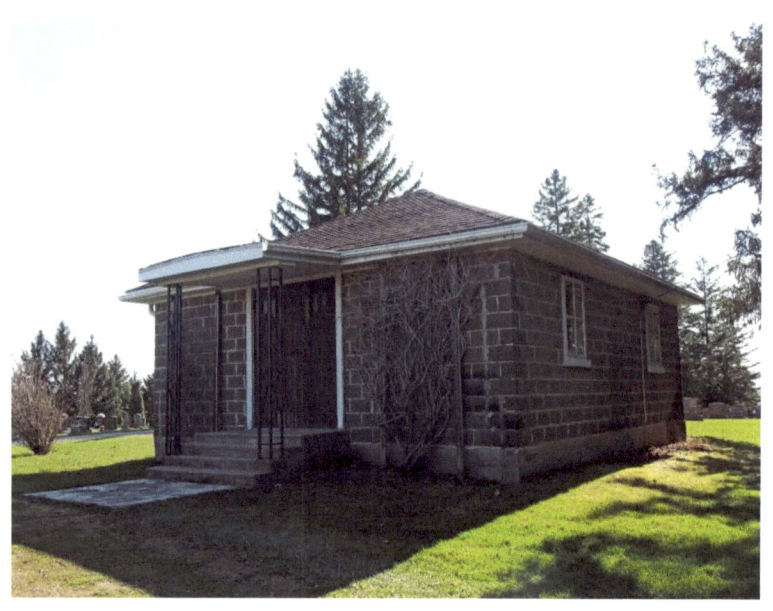

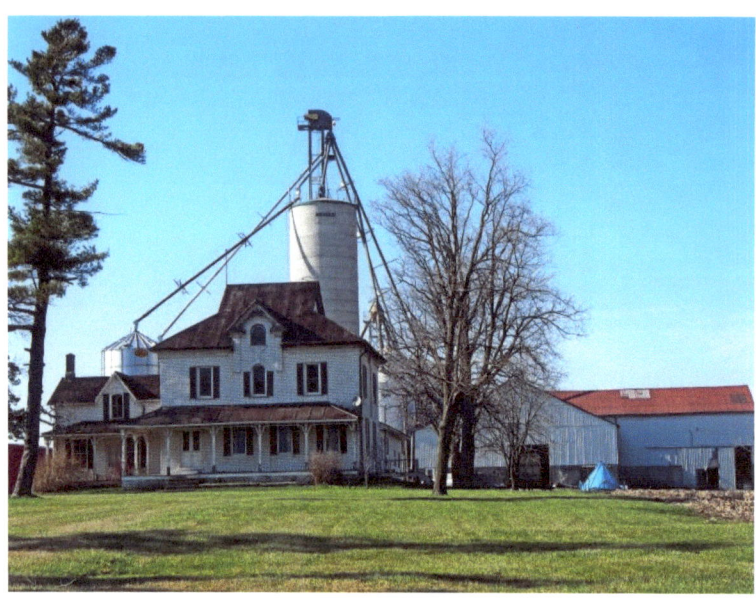

Windfall

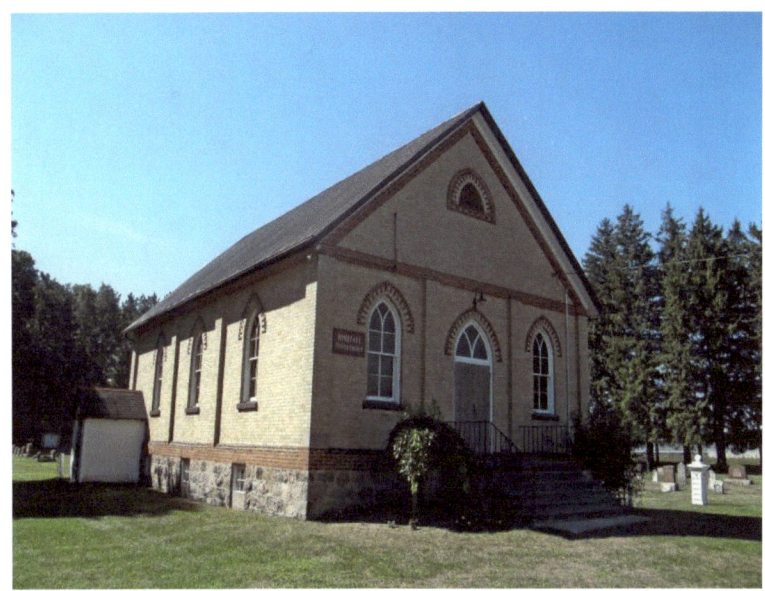

Windfall United Church – Oxford Road 29 - Originally United Brethren Church erected in 1899 – banding, dichromatic brickwork, lancet windows

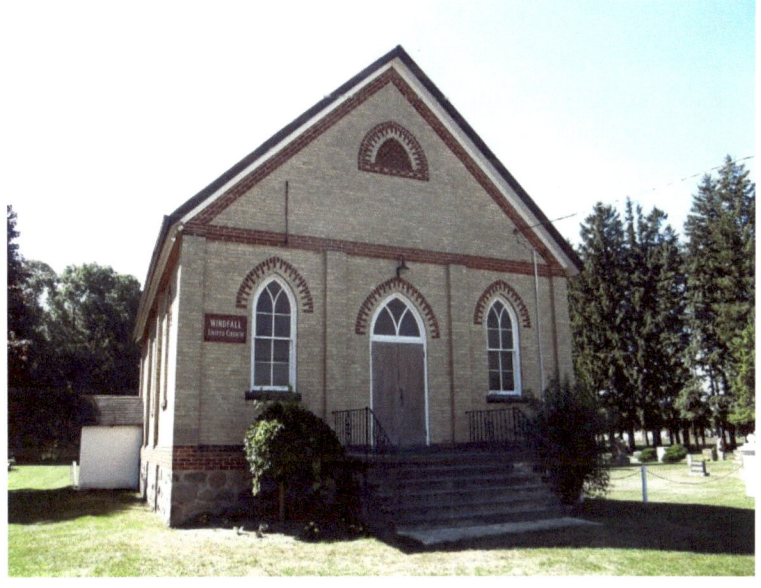

Ratho

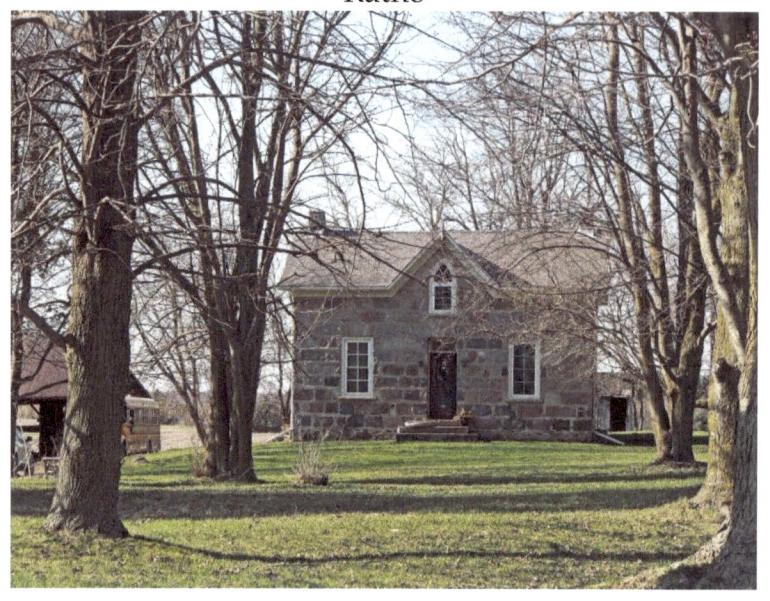

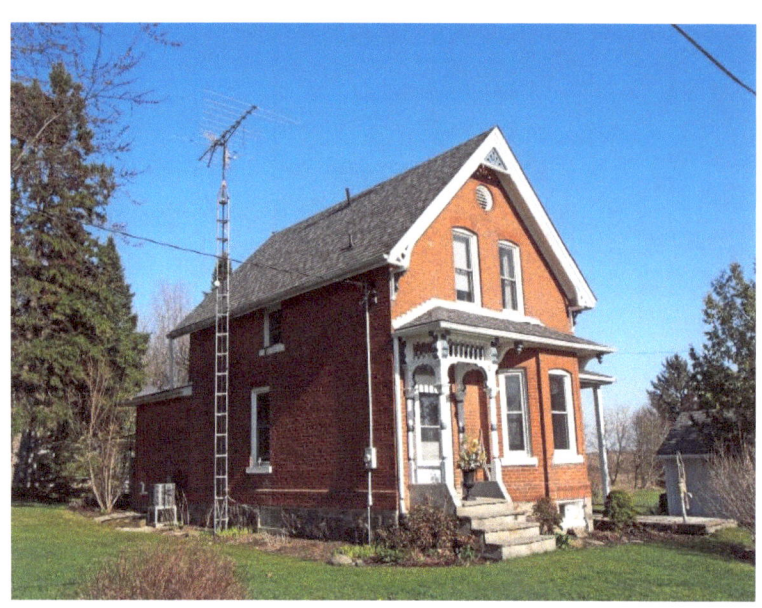

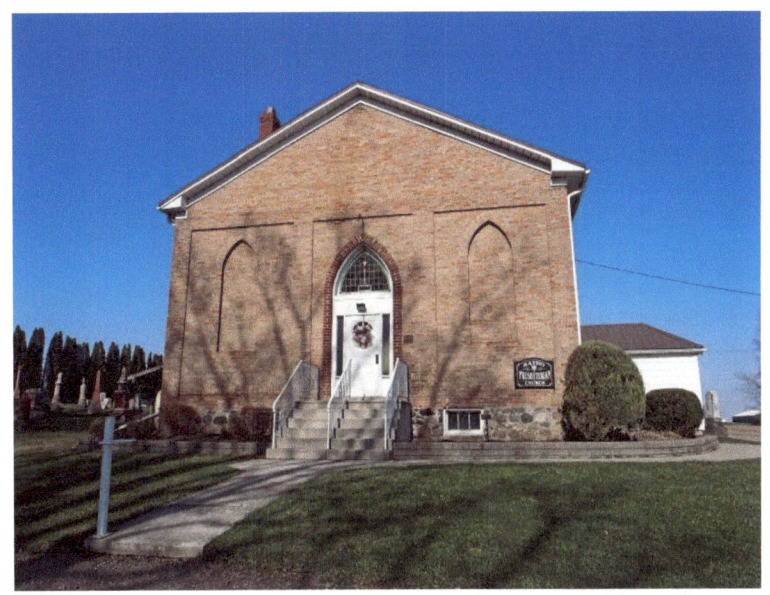

905987 Township Road 12 - Ratho Presbyterian Church

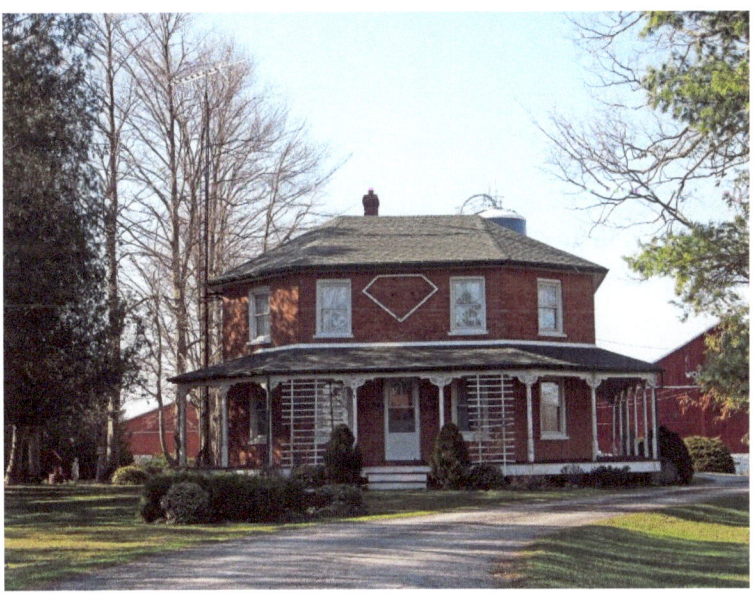

Architectural Terms

Battlement: A design for a parapet that has alternating solid parts and openings, originally used for defense, but later used as a decorative motif. Example: 15 Centre Street, Drumbo, Page 10	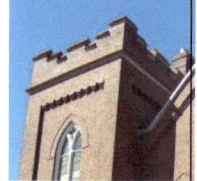
Bay Window: A window that projects out from a wall, in a semicircular, rectangular, or polygonal design. Used frequently in Gothic and Victorian designs. Example: #37, Plattsville, Page 36	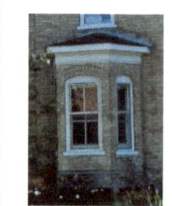
Brackets: a decorative or weight-bearing structural element which forms a right angle with one side against a wall and the other under a projecting surface such as an eave or roof. Example: Drumbo, Page 13	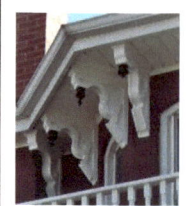
Keystones and Voussoirs: a voussoir is a wedge-shaped element used in building an arch. A keystone is the central stone that locks all the stones into position, allowing the arch to bear weight. A keystone is often enlarged and embellished. Example: Drumbo, Page 7	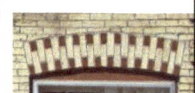
Lancet Window: a tall, narrow window with a pointed arch at its top. Example: 20 Pinkham Street, Drumbo, Page 10	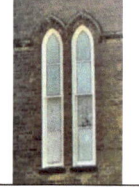

Palladian Window: a large window that is divided into three sections with the centre section larger than the two side sections and usually arched. Example: 23 Oxford Street, Drumbo, Page 18	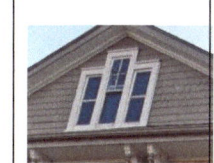
Pediment: a triangular section above the door or portico, usually supported by columns. The inside of the triangle is called the tympanum. Example: Drumbo, Page 13	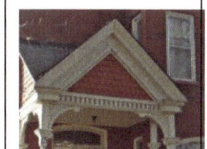
Quoin: masonry blocks at the corner of a wall, often a decorative feature, usually larger or of a different colour than the rest of the wall. Example: Drumbo, Page 12	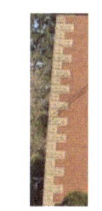
Sidelight: a vertical window that flanks a door, and is often used to emphasize the importance of a primary entrance. **Transom Window:** the light above the doorway, also called a fanlight. Example: Princeton, Page 29	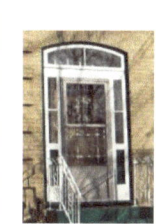
Verge board and Finial: also called bargeboards – hang from the projecting end of a roof and are often elaborately carved and ornamented. **Finial:** ornament added to the top of a gable, pinnacle, canopy or spire – a Gothic element. Example: #15, Drumbo, Page 13	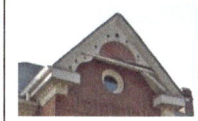

Building Styles

Gothic Revival, 1830-1890 – These decorative buildings have sharply-pitched gables with highly detailed verge boards, pointed-arch window openings, and dichromatic brickwork. It is a common style in Ontario. Example: Princeton, Page 23	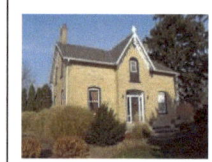
Italianate, 1850-1900 – A two story rectangular building with a mild hip roof, a projecting frontispiece, and generous eaves with ornate cornice brackets was the basis of the style; often there are large sash windows, quoins, ornate detailing on the windows, belvederes and wraparound verandahs. Italianate commercial buildings often have cast iron cresting and elegant window surrounds. Example: Drumbo, Page 13	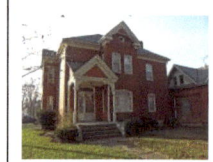
Regency Cottage, 1830-1860 – This style originated in England in 1815 and spread to Ontario later in the 19th century as British officers retired to Canada. It is a modest one-storey house with a low-pitched hip roof and has a symmetrical front façade. Example: Princeton, Page 31	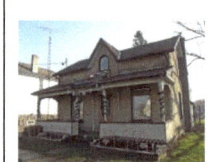

Other Books by Barbara Raue

Coins of Gold
Arrows, Indians and Love
The Life and Times of Barbara
The Cromwell Family Book
Laura Secord Discovered
Daddy Where Are You?

Montana Series
Book 1: Montana Dream
Book 2: Life on the Montana Frontier
Book 3: Montana to Boston and Back
Book 4: Montana Sons Go to War
Book 5: Montana Sons Return from War

© 2019 by Barbara Raue - All the photos in this book have been taken with my cameras. I own the rights to them.

This is a link to Barbara's website to view all of her books
http://barbararaue.ca

www.ingramcontent.com/pod-product-compliance
Lightning Source LLC
Chambersburg PA
CBHW040229220526
45473CB00001B/170